Ellen Terry

Joy Melville

Ellen Terry

HAUS
BOOKS
London

Copyright © Joy Melville 2006
Originally published in Great Britain by
Haus Publishing Limited
26 Cadogan Court
London SW3 3BX

The moral right of the author has been asserted

A CIP catalogue record for this book
is available from the British Library

ISBN 1-904950-14-0

Designed in Adobe InDesign and typeset in
Adobe Caslon Pro by Rick Fawcett

Printed and bound by Graphicom, Vicenza, Italy

Front cover: Getty Images
Back cover: National Trust Archive

www.hauspublishing.com

Contents

Ellen Terry was the most acclaimed, most loved and most highly paid actress in England in the late 19th century. Opening nights at the Lyceum Theatre, where she was Henry Irving's leading lady, brought carriages to a standstill. Postcards of her were bought in their thousands and young men's marriage proposals would begin, 'Well if Ellen Terry won't have me, will you?'

Introduction

Introduction

On 24th July 1928 a long winding funeral procession made its way through the country lanes of Kent accompanied by the joyous peal of church bells. Ellen Terry had said that she wanted 'no graveyard grimness' so the women mourners wore bright summer dresses and the men colourful ties. Haymakers and shepherds formed an impromptu guard of honour. It was a celebration of an extraordinary life.

Ellen Terry married three times: first, when she was only 17, to the renowned painter, G F Watts; secondly to the actor Charles Kelly; and thirdly at 60, to the actor James Carew, who at 34 was younger than her own son. She blithely shocked Victorian society by living with a lover by whom she had two illegitimate children. Within her circle, it was known she was having an affair with Henry Irving, her stage partner at London's Lyceum Theatre. Fortunately for her, there were no paparazzi then and her private life remained private—though Lewis Carroll once refused to introduce a young girl to her without the permission of the girl's parents.

Her son wrote a book claiming that there were two sides to Ellen Terry, both of which were at war with each other: the career actress and the doting mother. He was appalled when Ellen's intimate letters to Bernard Shaw were published but her daughter, instrumental in this, felt they would reveal the unseen side of Ellen: not the remote, adored icon but a feisty, witty and literate woman.

Ellen's prolific letters to all her friends were an extension of her character: spontaneous, articulate, funny and dramatic. They were full of capital letters, underlinings and exclamation marks. She signed herself according to her mood as ET, Ellen, Eleanora, Nell, Poor Nell, Nelly, Nellen, or whatever stage part she happened to be playing.

As an actress, like all distinguished performers, she took her work most seriously. Before playing Ophelia, she went to a 'madhouse' to study the inmates and she might study up to 25 reference books to get the character of a part correct. She believed the secret of good acting was the three 'I's': imagination, industry and intelligence.

Ellen was the ideal of every Pre-Raphaelite painter and had an extraordinary stage presence. Henry Irving called her 'a dream of beauty'; her friend Graham Robertson recalled her as Portia, with golden gown, golden hair and golden words, 'a dream of beautiful pictures in a scheme of gold'; and according to one viewer, even her last appearance on stage had an almost mystic quality: 'The vision of this fragile creature, far advanced in years, yet somehow not old, tremulously gliding across the stage with loving arms outstretched, all earthiness purged away by time, the spirit of beauty, rather than beauty itself, filled the spectators with a strange awe.'

Her constant tours throughout Britain made her a familiar face to thousands and at the height of her popularity she was mobbed in the streets. First nights at the Lyceum Theatre brought carriages to a standstill along the Strand. Her photographs were in magazines and papers, postcards of her were snapped up and young men in the 1880s used to propose to their girlfriends with the words, 'Well, as Ellen Terry won't marry me, will you?'

The actress Sara Siddons once terrified a shop assistant by the intensity with which she asked *Will it Wash?* Ellen Terry lived her life with equal intensity. She leaves an overwhelming impression of gaiety and fun—whether, on stage, puncturing Falstaff's padding with a pin or going through the city of Bath in an open carriage playing an imaginary tambourine. She was both Aphrodite, goddess of love and Boudicca the warrior queen: a thread of pagan gold weaving through the sombre morality of the Victorian era.

Acknowledgements

I have been helped by a great many people in writing this book. I would particularly like to thank Paul Meredith, Assistant Property Manager of the Ellen Terry Memorial Museum and Elizabeth Harrison; Sir Donald Sinden; Katharine Cockin, University of Hull; Claire Hudson, the Theatre Museum, London; Julia Rosenthal, Jeremy Mason, Margot Peters, Margaret Busby, Pauline Melville, the staff at the London Library and the Berg Collection, New York Public Library.

I am most grateful to the National Trust for permission to quote from letters held at the Ellen Terry Memorial Museum and to the Theatre Museum for permission to quote from letters held in their collection.

Prelude

Ellen Terry had been 17 for just three days when she danced down the aisle to marry the celebrated painter, G F Watts. Slim, with burnished red-gold hair and bursting with mischievous life, she mirrored youth and happiness. Her rich brown silk gown with ruched sleeves, designed by Holman Hunt, was covered by an exquisite Indian shawl and she wore a sprig of orange blossoms on her white quilted bonnet.

Her bridegroom was some 30 years older than she was. Today,

the age of 46 may seem relatively young, but Watts, with his long beard and floor-length outfit, shuffled rather than danced to the altar and gave an excellent imitation of being 86 rather than 46. Lady Constance Leslie, a guest at the wedding, remarked on the painful difference between the 'atrabilious' bridegroom, walking slowly and heavily up the aisle, and the 'radiant child bride dancing up it on winged feet.'

Their unlikely partnership came about after a mutual acquaintance, Tom Taylor, later editor of *Punch*, suggested Watts paint Ellen and her sister Kate, both acclaimed young actresses. Watts was immediately attracted to Ellen and in his double portrait of *The Sisters*, pale Kate slides into virtual anonymity whereas Ellen, leaning against Kate's shoulder, is painted with a passionate intensity, from the curve of her neck to her tip-tilted nose.

Ellen, in turn, was captivated by Little Holland House where Watts lived and worked and her youthful high-spirits, combined with her obvious admiration for him, further attracted Watts. Yet he did not appear an ardent lover. The Pre-Raphaelite painter Roddam Spencer-Stanhope, who knew Watts well, said Watts told a friend he was considering adopting Ellen Terry and asked his advice. 'I think she is too old,' was the reply. Watts raised the subject again, saying he was now thinking of marrying Ellen Terry. Back came the reply: 'I think she is too young.'

Nevertheless, Watts asked Ellen to be his wife and she accepted, delighted to be marrying the apostle of high art and leave her hard-working life behind her. Even on the morning of her wedding, she had first to bath and wash the hair of her younger brothers and sister—Floss, Charlie, Tom and baby Fred. By marrying, she could leave behind such family responsibilities and the drudgery of theatrical tours and move into an artistic paradise. She was becoming bored with the theatre and her career was not progressing.

It is ironic to think that Ellen Terry, who was to become England's most acclaimed and highly-paid actress, must have had one main thought in her head on the day she married. She would, thank God, no longer have to act.

Ellen was born in theatrical lodgings: indeed,
theatrical lodgings permeated the life of all
the young Terry children. They would even
sleep there, in bureau drawers, while
their parents acted in a nearby
theatre. There was no formal
training then for the theatre
in England: you gained your
experience by working in it.

Theatre T *In The Blood*

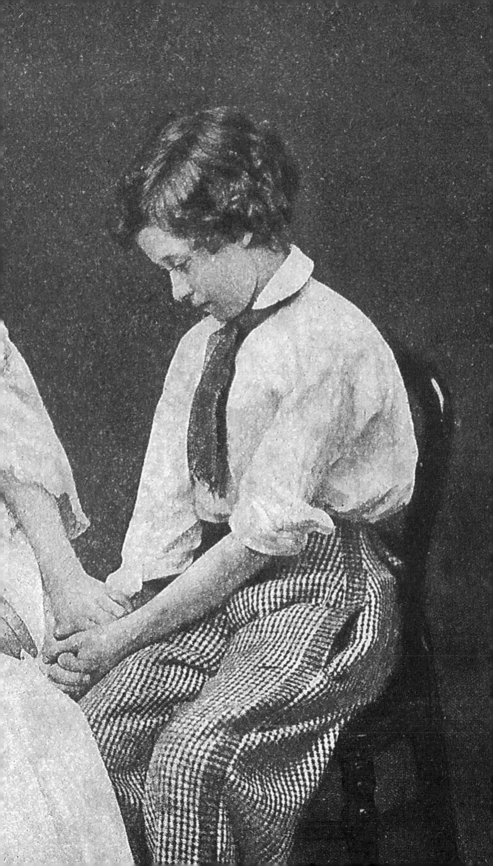

When the family was out of work Ellen's father staged his own theatricals. Here Ellen (right), with her elder sister Kate in Home for the Holidays *in which they played all the parts.*

Theatre in the blood

Ellen Terry diligently kept diaries. They were, she said, 'bursting, groaning dustbins of information, swelled by photographs, letters, telegrams, dried flowers.' Overwhelmed by their number and size she burnt most of them, then regretted it when writing her memoirs.

Her first memory was of jumping out of bed (fairly easy, this, as it was a mattress on the floor) to peer out of the window of an attic in Glasgow. Her actor parents, on tour in Scotland, had locked her in their lodgings for safety: her elder sister Kate was on stage with them at the theatre.

Theatrical lodgings permeated the early life of all the young Terry children. They would sleep there in bureau drawers, though Ellen recalled her mother, a devoted parent, also bundling up her babies in a shawl and putting them to sleep in her dressing room. When the children were a little older they were left in lodgings while their parents acted at the nearby theatre. Once these caught on fire and Ellen's mother 'rushed out of the theatre and up the street in an agony of terror. She got us out of the house all right, took us to the theatre, and went on with the next act as if nothing had happened.'[1]

Like most of the Terry children, Ellen was born in theatrical lodgings. The place was Market Street, Coventry and the date, 27th February 1847, despite her life-long conviction that she was born on that date a year later in 1848. Her parents, Ben and Sarah Terry, were strolling players: a romantic-sounding description

15

which disguised near-poverty. They had met in Portsmouth where Sarah, daughter of a Wesleyan lay preacher and a well-connected Scottish mother, became infatuated with Ben Terry, a handsome, ebullient Irish tearaway and son of a local Irish publican.

Ben was fanatically enthusiastic about the theatre, hanging about backstage and taking any job offered, such as drummer with the orchestra. Understandably, Sarah's parents were against their daughter marrying Ben, but she was now 21 and could flout their authority. The marriage took place on 1st September 1838, Ben having to lie about his age as he was still two weeks under 21.

With no settled job, the couple became travelling players. The biographer of the 19th century dramatist Charles Reade met the two Terrys on the Worcester Circuit and described Ben as a 'handsome, fine-looking, brown-haired man,' and Sarah as a 'tall, graceful creature with an abundance of fair hair, and with big blue eyes set in a charming face.'[2]

There was no formal training then for the theatre in England: you gained your experience by working in it. But Ben's enthusiasm and hard work turned him into an established supporting actor, while Sarah took minor supporting roles under the name of 'Miss Yerret' (Terry, spelt backwards) and also looked after the wardrobe. The life of a travelling player, walking from town to town, was hard and Sarah was frequently pregnant. She had eleven children in all. The eldest was called Ben after his father, followed by two daughters who died shortly after birth. Kate, born next, survived and Ellen was her fifth child.

Ellen was to say 'I can't even tell you when it was first decided that I was to go on the stage, but I expect it was when I was born, for in those days theatrical folk did not imagine that their children could do anything but follow their parents' profession.'[3] The Terrys' eldest girl, Kate, became a member of the troupe when she was only three years old. Kate's daughter later recalled that her mother did a turn, at that age, in a bonnet and shawl, singing a popular song of the time, *I'm ninety-five*. Ellen's memory differed: she recalls Kate, at three, dancing a hornpipe in a sailor's jumper, a tiny pair of white ducks and a rakish hat.

Ellen always regretted her own lack of formal schooling, education for children only becoming compulsory in 1876. Yet she considered that, outside from her profession, she had learned most from her environment. 'Perhaps it is this which makes me think environment is more important than education in forming character.'[4] In mid-Victorian England, most girls were taught at home by their mother or elder sisters and groomed only for marriage. Sarah made sure her daughters could cook and sew while Ben taught the children to sing and dance and declaim poetry.

Because of the emphasis at home on learning Shakespearian plays, Ellen and the other children were more literate than many others of their age. Ellen said that she and her sister Kate 'had the advantage of exceedingly clever and conscientious parents who spared no pains to bring out and perfect any talents we possessed.'[5]

Ellen's own first stage appearance was to have been in a Scottish pantomime as Spirit of the Mustard Pot. Aged eight, with a mass of fair hair, she seemed perfectly cast. But attempts to fit her into the property mustard pot failed dismally as she shrieked in pain. Her father, removing her, told her reproachfully that she would never make an actress. It was Kate who was regarded as having the talent and the better temperament. Ellen often heard her parents say, significantly, that they had no trouble with _Kate_.

They were certainly delighted when in 1852, Kate was offered the part of Prince Arthur in _King John_ in the actor-manager Charles Kean's company at the Princess's Theatre in Oxford Street in London. It meant, however, that the family had temporarily to split up: five-year-old Ellen stayed in Liverpool with her father, who was under contract there, while Sarah took Kate and her two sons (Ben and George) to lodgings in London. Kate proved a success and acted in Kean's company until he gave up managing it in 1859.

Ellen was always her father's favourite. He bequeathed her his light-heartedness and sanguine disposition and she said that, unlike her more conventional sister Kate, he liked her lawlessness. She cooked his breakfast and, away from her mother and Kate, she achieved a confidence and independence which stayed with her the rest of her life. She said of these months with her father that 'He never ceased teaching me to be useful, alert, and quick. Sometimes he hastened my perceptive powers with a slipper, and always he corrected me if I pronounced any word in a slipshod fashion. He himself was a beautiful elocutionist, and if I now speak my language well it is in no small degree due to my early training.'[6]

Within a year Ben Terry was also taken on by Kean and once more the family were together, living in the upper part of a house near Gower Street in London. Nine-year-old Ellen skipped onto the stage with her father and sister when she was given the part of the child Mamillius in *The Winter's Tale*. As Sarah was pregnant again (the child would be Marion), Ellen's salary was more than welcome. In return she received 6d a week in pocket money. The family, never able to afford a house before, moved into a small red-brick one in Stanhope Street near Euston.

It was Ellen's first role and she remembered the exhaustion of rehearsals, which began daily at ten in the morning including Sunday and frequently went on until the small hours. Sometimes her legs ached so much and she was so tired that she crept into the green-room and went to sleep. Kean always sat in the stalls with a clanging dinner-bell by his side and when anything went wrong on the stage, he rang it ferociously. Everything promptly stopped until his wife, who always sat on the side of the stage with her hair covered in a turban, set right what was wrong.

As Mamillius, Ellen was dressed in pink tights, a red and silver dress and wore her hair in sausage curls. She had to drag a little go-cart around the stage and on the first night, to her embarrassment, she tripped over it and fell flat on her back: 'A titter ran through the house, and I felt that my career as an actress was ruined for ever.' *The Times* the next day (1st May 1856) disagreed, considering her acting 'vivacious and precocious' and calling her a worthy relative of her sister. Dutton Cook, a contemporary critic, recalled in *Theatre Magazine* in June 1880 that 'She was a child of six or thereabout, slim and dainty of form, with profuse flaxen curls and delicately-featured face, curiously bright and arch of expression.'

Ellen played the part for 102 nights, never missing a performance to the annoyance of her understudy, and when Kean staged *A Midsummer Night's Dream* in the October of 1856 she was given the part of Puck. Ellen's memory of the play was of having a trap door accidentally slammed on her foot, breaking her toe. Mrs Kean rushed raise the trap door, whispering to Ellen 'Finish the

Ellen aged 9 in her first stage part as Mamillius in A Winter's Tale, *with Charles Kean. The production at the Princess's Theatre opened on 28th April 1856. Lewis Carroll considered that Ellen was a beautiful little creature 'who played with remarkable ease and spirit' while* The Times *declared she had played her part with vivacious precocity.*

19

Ellen pictured here in 1856, at the age of 9. She had been groomed for the stage by her father, Ben, of whom she said: 'He never ceased teaching me to be useful, alert, and quick. Sometimes he hastened my perceptive powers with a slipper, and always he corrected me if I pronounced any word in a slipshod fashion. If I now speak my language well, it is in no small degree due to my early training'.

play, dear, and I'll double your salary.' No true actress could resist that remark and Ellen wincingly continued on stage. Her salary was promptly raised from 15 to 30 shillings a week.

A Midsummer Night's Dream ran for a record 250 nights. Lewis Carroll called her 'the most perfectly graceful little fairy I ever saw', but Ellen remembered being gawky with prominent bright red cheeks. As well as relatively large parts, she also played a top-booted 'tiger' [the name for a youthful groom] in *If the Cap Fits* by Edmund Yates, the popular playwright, and a Worshipper of the Sun in *Pizarro*. More important, when she was not on stage, she watched from the wings, learning her trade.

Mrs Kean was an exacting teacher, telling the ladies of the company not to mix up their vowels like a pudding. 'If you want to say "I am going on the river" say it plainly and don't tell us you are going on the "rivah!"' When Ellen inherited Kate's part as Prince Arthur in *King John* in 1858 she couldn't do anything right and, with Mrs Kean storming at her and slapping her, broke down in tears. Full of mortification and grief, her voice unconsciously expressed what Mrs Kean wanted. Ellen remembered her saying, excitedly, 'That's right, that's right, you've got it! Now remember what you did with your voice, reproduce it, remember everything and do it!'[7]

What Ellen did remember was the view from the green-room window: 'It looked out on a great square courtyard, in which the spare scenery, that was not in immediate use, was stacked. For some reason or other this courtyard was a favourite playground for a large company of rats. I don't know what the attraction was for them, except that they may have liked nibbling the paint off the canvas. Out they used to troop in swarms, and I, from my perch on the window-seat, would watch and wonder. Once a terrible storm came on, and years after, at the Lyceum, the Brocken Scene in Faust brought back the scene to my mind—the thunder and lightning and the creatures crawling on every side, the greyness of the whole thing.'[8]

Ellen's acting career began at a time when the theatre was radically changing. Before the monarchy was restored in 1660, the Puritans had attempted to suppress drama altogether by outlawing theatre performances. The Licensing Act of 1737 restored the right to put on plays but issued patents, or licences, to just two London theatres: the Theatre Royal, Drury Lane, and the Theatre Royal, Covent Garden. Only these two were permitted to put on serious drama and new plays had to be approved by the Lord Chamberlain. Other theatres had to be licensed by magistrates for the performance of burlesques.

It was a fluid, confusing situation. The law was often ignored in the provinces while in London the burlesques gradually moved closer to the 'legitimate drama' staged at the two Theatres Royal. Playgoers expected good value for their money and a five-hour evening consisting of a play followed by a 'comedietta' or burlesque was quite usual, indeed expected. In 1843 an Act for Regulating the Theatres was passed, ending the licensing system. But by now theatres were bawdy and rowdy, shunned nervously by the middle and upper classes.

It was only due to outstanding actor managers, like Sir Squire and Lady Bancroft, Charles Kean and Henry Irving that the theatre became vibrant, respectable and offered serious drama. Without them, Ellen could well have spent her entire theatrical career playing boys in burlesques.

Leading theatres in London and the provinces always closed for the summer season, which lasted from July to September. During the summer of 1857 Ben Terry took his family to Rose Cottage in Ryde, the Isle of Wight, which he rented from his wife's sister. It was just a few miles from Portsmouth where he and Sarah had met and where his mother still lived. At Ryde he rented a small theatre and formed a family troupe consisting of himself, twelve-year-old Kate and nine-year-old Ellen. They did a number of sketches which proved popular enough for Ben to rent the theatre for further summer seasons. One critic called Ellen 'a perfect little heap of talent', but she admitted that 'a perfect little heap of vanity' would have been more accurate.

In 1859, Kean ended his run at the Princess's Theatre in order to go to America. It was a shock to the Terry family. Ben aside, Kate (now 14) had worked there since 1852 and Ellen (12) since 1856. Both girls were now well known in the London theatre. Dutton Cook said 'A peculiar dramatic sensitiveness and susceptibility from the first characterised the sisters Terry; their nervous organization, their mental impressibility and vivaciousness, not less than their personal charms and attractions, may be said to have ordained and determined their success upon the stage.'[9]

Ben took advantage of his daughters' popularity and as a way of earning money and continuing to act, devised an *Illustrative and Musical Drawing Room Entertainment.* The theatre bills advertised the young actresses as 'the original representatives of Ariel, Cordelia, Arthur, Puck, etc, which characters were acted by them upwards of 100 consecutive nights, and also before Her Most Gracious Majesty the Queen.' It sounded genteel enough to beckon in the middle-class audience and the first season took place in the Royal Colosseum in Regent's Park, in those days a favourite place for amusements of this description. It ran for 30 nights and proved highly popular, 30,000 paying for admission.

For the next two years, Ben took the show on tour to leading and smaller provincial towns. Sarah could now afford servants in the house to look after her the other children (Benjamin aged 21, George, ten, and the younger ones: Marion, Florence, Charles and the baby Tom), and there was enough money for school fees. She agreed to her husband's request and joined him and her two daughters on tour, taking occasional small parts. The four of them went off to Ryde for a short booking, then went as far afield as Dublin, Belfast, Plymouth, Exeter and Bristol. Ellen recalls the family walking from Bristol to Exeter, justifying the description of them as strolling players. They performed in a different place each day, earning about £10 to £15 a performance.

Kate and Ellen, like all young actors of the time, were expected to train in repertory, taking on a range of characters before appearing on the London stage. Repertory companies in those days offered a range of entertainment from farces to melodramas, sometimes doing several different plays or burlesques in a single week. Actors had to perform whatever part they were given. In 1861, after the tour, Ellen went with her father to London, putting her name down with a theatrical agent for work, but Kate was fortunate enough to be offered an engagement with James Henry Chute's company at the Theatre Royal, Bristol. It was regarded as one of the most excellent stock companies in England.

Ellen had been taken on by Madame Albina de Rhona, the manager of the Royalty Theatre in Soho. She had, recalled Ellen, 'nearly frightened me out of my wits at the first rehearsal by dancing round me on the stage in a perfect frenzy of anger at what she was pleased to call my stupidity.' Ellen, conscious of her large hands, would keep them tucked under her arms and Madame would scream at her to take them down: '*Mon dieu!* It is like an ugly young *poulet* going to roost!'[10]

After a year, Ellen joined Kate in James Chute's company in Bristol. Another actor in the company described Ellen as a 'girl of about 14, of tall figure, with a round, dimpled, laughing, mischievous face, a pair of merry, saucy, grey eyes, and an aureole of golden hair, which she wore, in the words of a modern ditty, "hanging down her back".'[11]

Although dwarfed by Kate's greater experience and superior roles, Ellen soon became a great favourite in Bristol playing 'Little Pickle' parts. Her popularity was largely due to her performances

23

in two of the Brough brothers' burlesques: *Endymion* and *Perseus and Andromeda*. Ellen played Cupid in *Endymion* and despite raised eyebrows at her scanty attire, her 'charm, her delightful grace and innate refinement, quite disarmed the prudes.'

Describing her acting in those days, the company actor said that her chief characteristic was a vivacious sauciness and that her voice already had some of the rich sympathetic quality which became 'one of her most distinctive charms.' Both Ellen and Kate had scores of admirers, devotedly following them to their morning rehearsals and waiting for them outside the stage-door at night. But the actor noted that Sarah Terry was a vigilant chaperone, always accompanying her daughters to and from the stage each night, and watching them from the wings the whole time.

Ellen was to say that the most important skill she learned when working for the company was to be 'useful' on stage: 'Not until we have learned to be useful can we afford to do what we like. The tragedian will always be a limited tragedian if he has not learned how to laugh. The comedian who cannot weep will never touch the highest levels of mirth.'[12]

It was while acting in Bristol that 15-year-old Ellen met 28-year-old Edward William Godwin, an ambitious architect and archaeologist who was later to play such a crucial role in her life. His wife Sarah was an attractive and cultured woman, who was deteriorating into chronic ill-health.

Godwin was obsessed by all the visual arts, had a passion for the theatre and contributed freelance *Theatrical Jottings* to the *Western Daily Press*. His designer's eye noticed the modern jewellery Kate wore with a classical costume and in a review for the paper on 30th October 1863, he commented equally critically, 'The younger Miss Terry's winning manner almost makes one ashamed to find fault, but some people would prefer to see *Cupid* standing occasionally on more than one leg, and not always smiling.'

Godwin was also Secretary of the Bristol Shakespeare Society and Ellen and Kate, with their parents' permission, used to go to the Godwins' house in Bristol, a large and attractive Georgian building, for the Shakespearean readings he organised. The interior design represented his aesthetic taste and advanced thinking: heavy Victorian furniture and wall-hangings were

Ellen in the part of Cupid in Endymion, *an extravaganza staged in 1862 by Mr J H Chute's acclaimed repertory company at the Theatre Royal, Bristol.*

replaced by plain coloured walls, Japanese prints, carefully chosen 18ᵗʰ-century antiques and polished floors.

Ellen was captivated by the place, 'with its Persian rugs, beautiful furniture, its organ, which for the first time I learned to love.' She said that 'its sense of design in every detail, was a revelation to

Ellen in 1865. She had left the stage the year before while playing Mary Meredith in Our American Cousin *at the Haymarket Theatre–saying she had acted the part 'vilely'. In fact she left to marry the painter G F Watts.*

me and the talk of its master and mistress made me think. At the theatre I was living in an atmosphere which was developing my powers as an actress and teaching me what work meant, but my mind had begun to grasp dimly and almost unconsciously that I must do something for myself...I now felt that I had never really lived at all before. For the first time I began to appreciate beauty, to observe, to feel the splendour of things, to aspire!'[13]

The two young actresses worked for the Chute company until 1863, when Chute opened the Theatre Royal, Bath. Ellen appeared there as Titania in *A Midsummer Night's Dream,* in a dress designed by Godwin. She and Kate returned to London, Kate to the Lyceum Theatre and Ellen to the Haymarket Theatre where she played Gertrude in *The Little Treasure.* Of this *The Times* critic wrote that the play presented Ellen in an entirely new light: 'Now she is matured into one of the happiest specimens of what the French call the *ingénue* that have been seen on any stage.'[14]

Ellen returned to Bristol for a brief engagement, but once back in London played Hero in *Much Ado About Nothing.* A critic called her 'graceful and winning.' She then played Julia in *The Rivals,* saying of her performance in later years, 'I think I could play it now, I certainly played it very ill then.' She considered that in her next part in *Our American Cousin,* she acted 'vilely.'

The critic Clement Scott said of her then, 'She was a young girl of enchanting loveliness. She was the ideal of every pre-Raphaelite painter and had hair, as De Musset says, *comme le blé.'*[15]

When *W**onderland went sour*

When 16-year-old Ellen Terry went to the studio of the acclaimed painter, G F Watts, she thought it was 'a Wonderland' and that Little Holland House where he lived was a paradise. It ignited her love of beauty and she was thrilled when Watts proposed. She was equally devastated when the marriage failed.

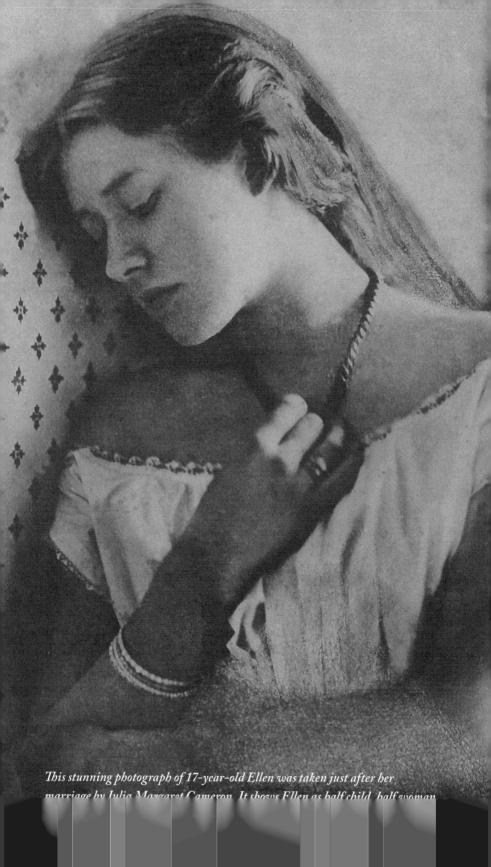

This stunning photograph of 17-year-old Ellen was taken just after her marriage by Julia Margaret Cameron. It shows Ellen as half child, half woman.

When wonderland went sour

Ellen explained her disenchantment with her acting by admitting that at the time she was 'preoccupied by events outside the theatre.' She and Kate, both now sought after socially, were friendly with Tom Taylor, playwright and later editor of *Punch*. It was he who had introduced the sisters to his circle of friends, one being the celebrated portrait painter, G F Watts. Taylor persuaded Sarah Terry that Kate, now considered one of London's leading young actresses, would be an excellent model for him. Sarah gave her permission but, busy with her younger children, could not act as chaperone and sent Ellen in her place.

The sittings for Watts took place in his studio in Little Holland House, west London. This large, rambling house was owned by Lord Holland who had let it to Thoby Prinsep, a retired civil servant from India, and his wife Sarah, who was the formidable sister of the equally formidable photographer, Julia Margaret Cameron.

Watts was 45 years old at the time. He had shown early talent in his drawing and spent much of his boyhood in the workshop of the sculptor, William Behnes. Watts had overwhelming confidence in his ability, which was just as well as when his father asked the President of the Royal Academy for his opinion of the boy's work, the President replied, 'I can see no reason why your son should take up the profession of art.'

Nevertheless, Watts was later to join the Royal Academy School and had had three portraits accepted for the summer exhibition by

31

the time he was 20. He was also getting commissions for portraits and won a £300 prize when he entered a mural contest to decorate the new Houses of Parliament. With the money he went to Italy, where he was introduced to Lord and Lady Holland. He stayed with them for four years, mostly painting commissioned portraits. It was work he despised as he preferred creating allegorical masterpieces. After they came back to England, Watts too returned.

However, once there he suffered a recurrence of his asthma, melancholy and migraine, saying miserably 'Often I sit among the ruins of my aspirations, watching the tide of time.' Lord Holland encouraged him to enter a competition for an oil painting for the House of Lords and this time he won £500; but his dreams of further success foundered. In depression he returned to commissioned portraits. Nevertheless, this brought him good fortune as while painting a portrait of the established beauty Virginia Pattle, he met her sister, Sarah Prinsep, who was acting as chaperone.

Sarah befriended him and became successor to the Hollands as his patroness. Admittedly she said of him, surely with acid in her voice, that 'He came to stay three days; he stayed 30 years' (she exaggerated, it was just 25 years). In reality she was delighted to have such a prestigious guest to show off at her weekly salons for writers and artists. She called him 'Signor', and organised a studio for him. His spirits rose, he grew a beard in keeping with his 'title' and began to paint with renewed vigour.

Watts's style of painting was to go out of fashion, but in his lifetime his moral and allegorical paintings like *Hope, Love Triumphant* and *Sir Galahad* were known all round England. *Hope,* in particular, became a popular icon, seen on the walls of parlours, schoolrooms and mission halls.

He had been living at Little Holland House for some ten years before meeting the two Terry sisters. It was probably shortly before 15th September 1862, which is when 18-year-old Kate and 15-year-old Ellen began a season at the Theatre Royal in Bristol. Kate at the time was the talk of London, after her lead performance in the play *Friends and Foes,* but Watts was at once strongly attracted to Ellen. Kate, Scott thought, was a pure English beauty, but Ellen was mystical and medieval.

G F Watts at the time he married Ellen. A wedding guest called him 'an atrabilious bridegroom' who walked 'slowly and heavily up the aisle'.

Watts initially painted a double portrait called *The Sisters*. Ellen was to sit for Watts many times, content in knowing that her face was the type which Watts loved to paint.

Indeed she willingly spent hours acting as model, saying after posing as Joan of Arc, that she remembered sitting in armour for hours and never realising that it was heavy until she fainted. Watts, who jumped at the noise of armour crashing down and splashed some red paint on the canvas, decided to keep it there to remind him to be more conscious of her stamina.

In writing of her visits there, Ellen was to say 'Little Holland

Ellen as a young wife: 'I was happy because my face was the type which the great artist who had married me loved to paint'.

House, where Mr Watts lived, seemed to me a paradise, where only beautiful things were allowed to come. All the women were graceful, and all the men were gifted.'[1] She was enchanted with the spacious rooms and wall frescoes by Watts: it ignited her love of beauty, originally sparked by Godwin. She called Watts's studio 'a wonderland.'

Watts strongly admired Ellen's beauty and on one occasion when Ellen was in his studio, he kissed her. In later years she wrote to Bernard Shaw to say that she would never forget her first kiss. 'I made myself such a donkey over it, and always laugh now when I remember. Mr Watts kissed me in the studio one day, but sweetly and gently, all tenderness and kindness, and then I was what they call "engaged" to him and all the rest of it, and my people hated it, and I was in Heaven for I knew I was to live with those pictures.'[2]

She added, in a passage suppressed when the Shaw-Terry letters were published: 'Then I got ill and had to stay at Holland House–and then–he kissed me–differently–not much differently but a little, and I told no one for a fortnight, but when I was alone with Mother one day she looked so pretty and sad and kind, I told her–what do you think I told the poor darling? I told her I must be married to him now because I was going to have a baby!!!! and she believed me!!'[3]

Although Ellen said her parents disliked the idea of the marriage, Tom Taylor enthusiastically promoted it. He successfully persuaded them it was a wonderful match for their daughter, allowing her to attain respectability and shed the disreputable aura around actresses.

Watts, aware of this, was anxious to 'rescue' Ellen from the stage. He wrote to his friend and confidant Lady Constance Leslie to say he was determined to remove Ellen 'from the temptations and abominations of the stage, giving her a [sic] education and if she continues to have the affection she now feels for me, marry her. There is a great difference between her age and mine. I should not think of putting any pressure upon her inclinations, but I think whatever the future brings, I can hardly regret taking the poor child out of her present life and fitting her for a better.

'I hope in what I had undertaking [sic] to do, I shall have the countenance of my friends, for it is no light matter from any point of view, even the expense will be considerable as I shall have to compensate her family for loss of her services… I should be v glad if you would tell Mrs Prinsep and her family so, for you know the prejudice there is against the stage (I share it myself). Miss Terry is very young and I do not see the future at all distinctly, but give her a chance of qualifying herself for a good position in society. I do not think I ought to be thought ill of… To make the poor Child what I wish her to be, will take a lot of time and most likely cost a great deal of trouble and I shall want the sympathy and aid of all my friends so I hope none will look coldly on my endeavours.'[4]

The painter Graham Robertson wrote to a friend in 1939 to say that 'If Watts thought he could mould that vital and radiant creature into what he wished her to be, he did not show much intelligence.'[5]

Sarah Prinsep was rumoured to be a prime instigator in promoting Watts's marriage to Ellen, but the above letter shows that Watts was worried about her reaction to the alliance. However, David Loshak, whose study of the relationship between Watts and Ellen appeared in *The Burlington Magazine*, considered that in no way was Watts a man who allowed others to run his life.[6]

It was understandable that Watts was anxious about Sarah Prinsep's reaction to the marriage as he was in no financial position to move out of Little Holland House and support Ellen himself. However, he met no real opposition as, in Sarah's eyes, Ellen was young and malleable and an ideal model for Watts.

Watts had a very prolific painting period while married to Ellen. He was inspired by Ellen as a model: she personified his abstract ideals of goodness and innocence. His celebrated sensuous painting of her wearing her wedding dress, called *Choosing*, showed her cupping to her face a camellia blossom (a symbol of worldly vanities which the young actress was leaving), while holding in her other hand some violets (a symbol of innocence and simplicity).

A great deal of amused and inventive gossip about the marriage took place. The subject came up at the weekly lunch at *Punch* magazine, for instance, and Henry Silver, a staff member who kept a diary of the conversations there, noted 'apropos of Old Watts marrying Miss Ellen Terry—who really loves him. She received as a Valentine the ashes of her photographs, burned by an admirer—"Bly fool!" bursts out Shirley (Brooks, who later became editor)'.[7]

One focal point of gossip was precisely how the marriage came about. The novelist Violet Hunt claimed that 'my mother always said that Kate went to him (Watts) and said that he had made her "poor little sister dead in love with him" and Nelly was awed and impressed by the magnificence of being Mrs Watts.'[8]

The marriage, small and quiet, took place at St Barnabas's Church, Kensington, on 20th February 1864. There was a natural scepticism about the outcome of the partnership, given two such different characters—Watts with his asthma and depressive nature and the 'child-bride' Ellen, with her impulsiveness, unpredictability and bubbling high spirits. Watts's professorial attitude continued at the wedding. When Ellen wept copiously during the service, he merely said, 'Don't cry. It makes your nose swell.'

Hebe Elsna in her romantic novel about Ellen, Watts and Godwin, *The Sweet Lost Years*, had Watts trembling violently on the first night of his marriage, backing away from the marriage bed and telling Sarah Prinsep: 'Nell is so innocent, so virginal—she knows nothing. She would be repelled, horrified, and lost to me. All that I prize in her as a model would be defiled.'[9]

Marguerite Steen, a friend of the Terry family, claimed that after the marriage 'The ill-matched pair went back to Little Holland House. On her marriage night Nelly was discovered, crying bitterly, on the staircase outside the nuptial chamber. Her initiation, at the hands of a fumbling and neurotic lover, was a sad one.'[10]

However, conjectures about the sexual side of the couple's marriage are just that: conjectures. David Loshak stated in the *Burlington Magazine* that no one could possibly know the truth. He considered that Watts felt passion for Ellen as well as compassion, citing as an example his picturing of nude Ellen as Francesca da Rimini, clasped in her lover's arms, in his painting of Paola and Francesca. Wilfrid Blunt, in reply, queried Loshak's contention that Watts, prior to his marriage, had abstained from sex for many years, asking in turn how this could be known. Blunt agreed with the view that Watts was repressed and shy of sex all his life and believed the veiled eroticism of some of his paintings supported this hypothesis.[11]

The Prinseps took Ellen and Watts for a honeymoon visit to stay with Sarah's sister, Julia Margaret Cameron, and her husband at their house at Freshwater on the Isle of Wight. Mrs Cameron photographed Ellen in the bathroom of Lord Tennyson's nearby house, producing an unforgettable picture of a young girl verging on womanhood. Watts's portraits of Ellen also had a moving, romantic intensity to them, an air of enchantment.

The Camerons often visited Lord Tennyson and his family and Ellen, after one visit, said: 'I was still so young that I preferred playing Indians and Knights of the Round Table with Tennyson's sons, Hallam and Lionel, and the young Camerons, to sitting indoors noticing what the poet did and said… he and all the others seemed to me very old. There were my young knights waiting for me; and jumping gates, climbing trees, and running paper-chases are pleasant when one is young.' She admitted, however, that she loved listening to Tennyson reciting poetry, particularly the Ride from Ghent to Aix, which appealed to her dramatic sense. 'He used to preserve the monotonous rhythm of the galloping horses in Browning's poem, and made the words come out sharply like hoofs upon a road.'[12]

Ellen's youthful behaviour was worlds away from Watts's gravitas. She was in an impossible situation. Although loving the world of Little Holland House and indeed Watts himself, she needed far more attention and consideration from him to help her grow to maturity as his wife. Watts was too busy in his studio, preferring to paint rather than instruct Ellen. He found her demands intrusive and shying away from emotion, both by day and night, retreated further into his studio. Ellen had no role as his wife. Mrs Prinsep, who capably ran the household, naturally had no intention of relinquishing her position.

Ellen was all too conscious of not being accorded the status of Mrs Watts at the weekly salons hosted by Mrs Prinsep, admitting she 'sat, shrinking and timid, in a corner—the girl-wife of a famous painter. I was, if I was anything at all, more of a curiosity, a side-show, than hostess to these distinguished visitors.'[13]

The painter Roddam Spencer-Stanhope agreed that Mrs Prinsep 'never ceased to treat Ellen as a naughty child who must be scolded and made obedient, and a high-spirited, unconventional girl naturally resented this treatment, while Watts, absorbed in his art, was little aware of the mischief which was preparing.'[14]

Mrs Prinsep's attitude was illustrated at a lunch party at which Ellen Terry, then a new bride, was present. Roddam Spencer-Stanhope's wife was there and described Ellen as being strikingly lovely, with brilliant eyes and very beautiful hair, 'but quite a schoolgirl and a decided tomboy.' After lunch, while Watts paced to and fro in the garden talking, Mrs Spencer-Stanhope remained with Mrs Prinsep and Ellen in the drawing room.

'Suddenly the latter, with an air of supreme boredom, leant back over the arm of a chair in which she was seated, and, shaking her head to and fro, loosened the pins from her hair which tumbled about her shoulders like a cloak of shining gold. My aunt could only gaze in delight at the beauty of the girl as she sat there swaying her head gently from side to side while the mass of shimmering hair shrouded her and swept the floor. But Mrs Prinsep was horrified. "Ellen! Ellen!" she cried, "put up your hair instantly!" And Ellen, flashing a wrathful glance at her tormentor, grasped the waving mass of gold, coiled it carelessly upon her head, and, stabbing it with pins, sat there looking lovelier than ever, a petulant, scolded child.'[15]

Related to the dignified Watts, such behaviour so upset him that he could scarcely work. Loshak claimed he was 'too indecisive to do anything about it', and it was generally thought that Mrs Prinsep, not he, organised the separation.

Ellen was to say that during her marriage she never had a single regret for having left the theatre. 'I wondered at the new life,' she said, 'and worshipped it because of its beauty. When it suddenly came to an end, I was thunderstruck; and refused at first to consent to the separation, which was arranged for me in much the same way as my marriage had been.'[16]

Lewis Carroll, who was intent on meeting the Terry family paid several visits to their house in Stanhope Street and on 21st December 1864 finally met Ellen, 'the one I have always most wished to meet of the family...I was very much pleased with what I saw of Mrs Watts—lively and pleasant, almost childish in her fun, but perfectly ladylike.'[17]

If Ellen was showing her usual sense of fun, she must have been disguising any feelings of loss as the deed of separation between herself and Watts was drawn up a mere month later on 26th January 1865.

The fact that her marriage had lasted less than a year before Watts returned her to her parents like an unwanted parcel, naturally raises conjecture. Possibly Watts was disillusioned, having chosen Ellen for his wife because she was the opposite of his mature, masterful woman friends like Mrs Prinsep and Mrs Cameron, only to find that Ellen had an equally strong-willed personality. David Loshak considers this theory 'an important cause of the marriage's failure, of greater consequence than the interference of the Pattle sisters' (i.e., Sarah Prinsep and Julia Margaret Cameron).[18]

The deed of separation stated that 'unhappily differences have arisen and still exist' between the two participants. Watts agreed to pay Ellen £300 a year 'so long as she shall lead a chaste life.' If she returned to the stage, this amount would be reduced to £120 a year. Watts was obviously still intent on removing her from temptation. She, in turn, had to promise not to 'molest or disturb the said G F Watts in his person or manner of living…or seek or endeavour to compel the said G F Watts to cohabit with her or to compel any restitution of conjugal rights.' That sounds like a frightened man.

Ellen said that she had never contradicted the inaccurate stories of her married life because 'they were so manifestly absurd.' In the *Divorce Proceedings* (High Court of Justice, Probate, Divorce and Admiralty Division), which took place 12 long years later on 13th March 1877, Watts claimed:

'That although considerably older than his intended wife he admired her very much and hoped to influence, guide and cultivate a very artistic and peculiar nature and to remove an impulsive young girl from the dangers and temptations of the stage.

'That very soon after his marriage he found how great an error he had made. Linked to a most restless and impetuous nature accustomed from the very earliest childhood to the stage and forming her ideas of life from the exaggerated romance of sensational plays, from whose acquired habits a quiet life was intolerable and even impossible, demands were made upon him he could not meet without giving up all the professional aims his life had been devoted to.

'That he did not impute any immorality at that time but there was an insane excitability indulging in the wildest suspicions, accusations and denunciations driving him to the verge of desperation and separation became absolutely necessary unless he gave up his professional pursuits which was out of the question as he had no independent means and it was arranged by his friends and those of his wife that a separation should take place. That separation took place within a year of his marriage...

'That the matter pained him very much and that he refused to go into Society altogether and gave himself up entirely to study and close pursuit of his profession.'

Ellen may have been light-heartedly impetuous, but surely cannot be accused of 'insane excitability'? Watts's lawyer, in drawing up this document, sounds like a penny-dreadful novelist.

Violet Hunt reflected such claims in her assertion (given without revealing her source) that 'Old Mrs Prinsep (was) the real demon of the piece...she first got the great Watts (Signor) to share her roof and shine on her with reflected glory, then...(to) keep him she conceived the idea of marrying him off to Nelly Terry, a rather simple little innocent flirt whom Tom T. had brought to the house...She did not realise that Mrs Prinsep meant to keep him and did.'[19]

Years later, in 1888, while Ellen was on tour in Chicago, she heard of the death of Sarah Prinsep. In a letter to her sister, Kate, dated 10th January 1888, she wrote: 'Just fancy Mrs Prinsep dead: that healthy hale woman—I think she was pretty cruel, or stupid more like, to me—but I suppose all's for the best and I know she was sorry afterwards.'[20]

Taking this, together with a letter written to a friend, Mary-Anne Hall on 3rd February 1865, just after the separation, Ellen apparently held Mrs Prinsep responsible for the end of her marriage. She ended her letter to Mary-Anne, 'Your very loving friend, Ellen Alice Watts. NB. Better known as "Poor Nell".' She then added '"Ah me I am aweary, and I wish that I were dead." No dear Marion I have much to live for even now. "Nil Desperandum" is my motto. I have youth (I'm not very old rather) and I have great great hope—Oh! so much and I can't believe that all is lost yet—Share Faith too dear, for I cannot but think that help will, must come to me some day. Hope—Faith—Two great things—but Charity! Ah! Ellen, Ellen I'm afraid you have not one particle of that, the most beautiful of all, all, feelings or you wd not feel as you do towards a person of flesh and blood and that person a Woman. God forgive her for I cannot do so—I suppose I am very,

very wicked to feel so but indeed Marion I think and think what have I done that she sd. use me so—God knows I'd forgive anyone that even killed me if I loved them. But "hope on hope ever" and don't be selfish Nelly—you are talking to yourself! Pray forgive me, for this is selfishness.

'I believe the great business of life is to be merry and wise—and the best way to keep up one's self is to go out, to learn the sorrow and troubles of others which must make one forget one's own... to relax the ugliness of those furrows and wrinkles which sorrow ploughs in the fair forehead of God's creation. Oh! What an "idiot" I am.'[21]

A few weeks later she wrote again to say, 'My old face looks like a tallow candle, only there's not so much colour in it—and I am in such bad spirits and can't account for it.'

Ellen was undoubtedly bewildered at the abrupt end to her marriage. Amid all the rumours, she wrote a surprisingly unbiased account in her memoirs, but claimed that 'the whole thing was managed by those kind friends whose chief business in life seems to be the care of others...There were no vulgar accusations on either side, and the words I read in the deed of separation, "incompatibility of temper"—a mere legal phrase—more than covered the ground. Truer still would have been "incompatibility of occupation" and the interference of well-meaning friends..."The marriage was not a happy one," they will probably say after my death, and I forestall them by saying that it in many ways was very happy indeed. What bitterness there was effaced itself in a very remarkable way.'[22]

She was later to write some generous comments in her copy of G K Chesterton's book on Watts, published by Duckworth in 1904, the year of Watts's death. When Chesterton mentions with amusement a self-portrait by Watts at 19, with 'flowing and voluminous dark hair' which makes him easily 'mistaken for an advertisement of a hairdresser, or by the more malicious, for a minor poet,' Ellen writes 'but he was just a boy then.' And Chesterton's comment that Watts's 'famous skull cap, which makes him look like a Venetian senator, is as pictorial and effective as the boyish mane in the picture' has Ellen's explanatory scrawl next to it saying, 'He wore it because the slightest draught gave him excruciating pain in his head.' On Watts's unsuccessful request to decorate Euston, Ellen wrote: 'Dull as it is now, it wd have been glorified by Watts.'[23] On his death, she said that because of his wonderful work, he should be buried in Westminster Abbey.

Nevertheless, at the time her anger with Mrs Prinsep changed direction and was vented on Watts. In another letter to Mary-Ann Hall, written from Settle in north Yorkshire presumably around this same time, Ellen's emotions got the better of her: underlinings and exclamation marks litter it. At the top she has written, 'Do not mention what I've written to you to anyone else, please' and goes on to say that the dark cloud over her life has now been lifted, that she had found some new friends, was at last contented and that what happened to her had at least taught her patience. But her words show the past still rankled:

'I bear no malice but I feel no love toward Mr Watts—He is to me now as if he did not exist! I daresay you will wonder what has changed my feelings so completely. I'll tell you—reports meet me on every side down here in this quiet place—in Manchester—and all about of what Mr Watts has said of me—all most cowardly —and most untrue!! There is no shadow of doubt (for it has been proved to me) that he and not Mrs Prinsep only has said these things!! (I cd have forgiven the spite, and vexation of an angry and not good woman) but not the untruths of one whose constant care was to make every one think me untruthful and one to whom I was devoted heart and soul—and for one I tried to make fond of me by every power I cd think of and for whom I wd not have left (if all the world had wished it) had he not desired it also—although I thought at the time it would be my death. But enough of this wild way of talking, suffice it that Mr Watts has now become to me a mere ordinary person who has been, once upon a time a source of the only unhappiness I ever felt.'

Ellen went on to say that she entirely forgave Watts as he had bad advisers, and emphasised to her friend that Watts had not brought any charge against her that 'says I was not true to him in every way, and that I didn't do my best to please him, but he simply says he could not live with me!'...the one unhappiness I had (my love for him—which was quite thrown away) has left me also...'[24]

To be sent home because your husband announces he cannot live with you is demeaning, to say the least. It is no wonder that Ellen's emotions were turbulent, particularly as she could see no reason for her rejection and sought someone to blame. However she admitted that at the time, despite being so upset, she showed as little rebellion as a sheep. 'But I was miserable, indignant, unable to understand that there could be any justice in what had happened.'

Lady Duff Gordon claimed Ellen told her that she had visited Godwin one evening only to find him very ill in bed, whereupon she stayed the night to make poultices and look after him, saying 'I never even thought of the conventions or the construction that might be placed on my actions.' She returned home to find her husband and parents waiting for her 'utterly horrified at what I had done in all innocence.'[25]

An earlier biographer of Ellen Terry, Roger Manvell, dismissed this story as moonshine and indeed Lady Duff Gordon's memoirs were not published until 1932, some 70 years after the event. There was no accusation of misconduct during the marriage in the formal divorce petition 12 years later. However, the story had gained enough credence to be mentioned by Ellen's daughter who said, in her notes on her mother's memoirs, that this 'indiscretion' had 'led to a domestic scene, that often-acted scene which ends in a door being slammed on an erring daughter.'[26]

After the separation, Ellen only met Watts once face-to-face. He told her she had grown.

Having been so enraptured with the culture to which she had been introduced, Ellen loathed having to return to her parents, once more 'a daughter', embarrassing proof of her failure as a wife. 'Mother furnished a room for me and I thought the furniture hideous. Poor mother! For years, Beethoven always reminded me of mending stockings, because I used to struggle with the large holes in my brothers' stockings upstairs in that ugly room, while downstairs Kate played the *Moonlight Sonata*. I caught up the stitches in time to the notes!' For Ellen, the future looked bleak. 'This was the period when, though everyone was kind, I hated my life, hated everyone and everything in the world more than at any time before or since.'[27]

MISS ELLEN TERRY.

COPYRIGHT.

A pensive Ellen in 1866 after her marriage break-up. Watts paid her £300 annually, 'so long as she shall lead a chaste life'.

Her misery was marginally alleviated by a visit to Paris where she saw Sarah Bernhardt act, loved the city's 'nonchalant gaiety' and became 'dead sick' of all the galleries in the Louvre. When she returned to England and ultimately acting, she did so only half-heartedly. It was hardly surprising: there was little for her to do at her parents' home. Lewis Carroll paid a visit to the Terry house on 7th April 1865, and saw Ellen playing and singing with the family. In July of that year he photographed them all and the picture he took of Ellen shows her looking pensive and sad.

Ellen's annual payment of £300 from Watts meant that she no longer had to act to earn her living. She made one guest appearance on 29th June 1866 to support a benefit performance for Kate, playing Helen in Sheridan Knowles's *The Hunchback*. She was worried about doing so as the part she was playing was not that of a 'desirable' person and she was concerned people might confuse the character with her. She was praised for it, but said she cared nothing about her success. 'I was feeling wretchedly ill, and angry, too, because they insisted on putting my married name on the bills.'

She made occasional stage appearances. Lewis Carroll, for example, saw her in a single performance of Tom Taylor's *A Sheep in Wolf's Clothing* on 11th May 1867, in which she appeared with Kate. It was one of Kate's last performances as in the October of that year she achieved social success by marrying Arthur Lewis, a partner in the wealthy silk mercer business, Lewis and Allenby of Regent Street. He flouted his mother's wishes in doing so as she was passionately against the match, considering actresses immoral. Kate Terry had been an immensely popular actress. Ellen said that she looked like a frail white azalea on stage, but assessed her sister's acting as being scientific: 'There was more ideality than passionate womanliness in her interpretations.' By Kate's retirement from the stage, she left the field open to Ellen to perpetuate the Terry name.

Ellen was young and active and despite her lack of interest she finally resumed her stage career, appearing in another of Tom Taylor's plays, *The Antipodes: or the Ups and Downs of Life* at the Theatre Royal, Holborn on 8th June 1867. She claimed she was practically driven back to the stage by Tom Taylor, her father and mother, and others who meant to be kind. 'They looked ahead and saw clearly it was for my good.' The play, however, was not a success.

A triumvirate of playwrights—Tom Taylor, Dion Boucicault and Charles Reade—were dominant in producing current plays. Their output and energy was extraordinary and together they did much to resuscitate the flagging English theatre.

Mr and Mrs Alfred Wigan took over the management of the new Queen's Theatre in London in October 1867 and offered Ellen an engagement. Mrs Wigan, like Mrs Kean, affectionately bullied Ellen about her acting. Ellen had a habit of restlessly moving around the stage and at rehearsals Mrs Wigan would shout from the stalls 'Stand still. Now you're of value. Motionless! just as you are! That's right.' If Ellen laughed on stage, she would hear a loud hiss of anger coming from the stage box. 'I was simply paralysed with terror,' she said.

Ellen then played a succession of vapid parts, none of which was memorable. It was, however, in one of these, a version of Shakespeare's *Taming of the Shrew* staged in December 1867, that Ellen's leading man was the ambitious Henry Irving. It was their first meeting and she discovered he thought her 'charming and individual as a woman but as an actress hoydenish.' She in turn was impressed by his 'fierce and indomitable will' and the way he thought and cared for nothing but work. 'Yet he played badly, nearly as badly as I did; and how much more to blame I was, for I was at this time much more easy and skilful from a purely technical point of view.'[28] Another reason she gave for not acting well herself was being 'a woman who was at this time caring more about love and life than the theatre.' The play was understandably panned and was swiftly withdrawn.

Ellen only appeared in one more play, *The Household Fairy* at the Queen's Theatre, in February 1868. 'Soon afterwards,' she wrote in her memoirs, 'I left the stage for six years, without the slightest idea of ever going back. I left it without regret.'

This was the second time within a few years that Ellen had left the stage without a hint of regret. She was not then, or at any time in her life, ambitious, pretentious or conceited about her talent. The stage for her was simply a way of earning a living.

The ℱ *world well lost for love*

Ellen was 21 when she defied society
and went to live with the architect and
designer, Edward Godwin, in a cottage
in Hertfordshire. Her view of the
countryside was romantic and she adored
the two children she was to have. She was
unaware that her lack of organisation and
domesticity was contributing to Godwin's

Ellen in 1873 in the house where she lived with Edward Godwin. Godwin, an architect and designer, had decided views on clothes and interior decoration. The walls of their house were often plain with Japanese paper curtains and he liked Ellen to wear aesthetically-fashionable Japanese-style clothes.

The world well lost for love

Ellen not only left the stage at 21, she vanished secretly, without a word to anyone, either unaware or uncaring of her parents' and friends' reaction. Her parents had thought she had a great future on the stage and were left shocked and bewildered by her disappearance and the apparent end to her career. Ellen's younger brothers and sisters were still at school and for the first time, in the large Terry family, there was no young Terry on the stage. It was probably because she knew her parents would totally oppose her plans that Ellen hid the truth from them.

Not knowing what had happened to her, Ellen's parents were traumatised when a body of a girl who looked startlingly like Ellen was dredged up from the river. Her father identified the body as hers and her sisters, at boarding school, were put into mourning. Her mother then viewed the body and denied it was Ellen. In a renewed attempt to find her, Tom Taylor was asked to assist in the search. Ellen, hearing of the discovery of the body, 'flew up to London to give ocular proof to my poor distracted parents that I was alive.'

Taylor's wife, told of Ellen's reappearance, wrote sharply to her husband to say that she was more sorry than surprised to hear of Ellen's behaviour, 'though I should not have expected that she would have shown her vice in so hard and uninteresting a way.' She half excused this 'vice' on the grounds that Ellen must have been feeling 'reckless and forlorn,' but could not understand why her husband was ever called in to help trace her. 'Why we never

Edward Godwin–for the love of whom 21-year-old Ellen threw caution to the winds and daringly went to live with him in a Hertfordshire cottage. It resulted in ostracism by Victorian society.

once thought of Mr Godwin! Certainly I did not.'[1]

For almost as shocking as the apparent news of Ellen's death was the discovery of her 'vice'—which was that she was now living with Edward Godwin, the architect whose house she had so admired in Bristol when she and Kate took part in Shakespearean readings.

Despite her parents being delighted to find she was still alive, she was, in Victorian parlance, still lost to them. Her behaviour in going to live with Godwin caused a total breach between Ellen and her family. Her sister, Kate, now living a highly respectable life with her new husband, refused to receive Ellen at her house.

Although Godwin was now a widower, Ellen was not divorced from G F Watts. She and Godwin outrageously and uncaringly flouted Victorian conventions by living together, unmarried, in a small cottage near Wheathampstead in Hertfordshire.

Exactly how and when Ellen had met Godwin again after her marriage, or its breakdown, is unclear. But Godwin almost certainly moved in her circles during his frequent visits to London from Bristol. Although an architect by profession, he had a passion for design in all areas: the interior design of buildings and the design of furniture, decoration and even clothes. He was also an ardent lover of Shakespeare and the theatre, which might have revived his friendship with Ellen. Or he could have met her at the house in Lavender Sweep, Clapham, south London, where Tom Taylor and his wife lived, as Mrs Taylor knew him. Everyone of note went there as Tom Taylor, being dramatic and art critic for *The Times, Punch* writer and a busy playwright, had a huge circle of friends.

Ellen and Kate had long been frequent visitors, and Ellen said that it was there that despite their lack of formal education, 'we were educated.' The Taylors, she said, always welcomed them 'and every Sunday we heard music and met interesting people—Charles Reade among them.' However, if she did meet Godwin there on various occasions, their burgeoning friendship must have been very discreet as Mrs Taylor was obviously surprised to hear that Ellen was with him. No one had thought of Godwin being involved.

Godwin was now 35 years old, sophisticated, erudite and talented. He had deep-set eyes, a rakish black beard and a dandyish black broad-brimmed hat. His knowledge of the arts was impressive and he was an amusing conversationalist. As a result both he and his work were much in demand. Although trained as a Gothic Revival architect, he was one of the most forward-looking designers of the late 19th century and at the forefront in introducing Japanese influence into European design. He designed some extraordinarily brilliant textiles, tiles and wallpapers, sharing many of the same ideas as William Morris and he was also involved in theatre design and dress reform.

Early in 1864 he had formed a partnership in Bristol with his friend and fellow architect, Henry Crisp, in which his part was to submit designs for various architectural competitions. (It was in Crisp's house, when Ellen was acting in Bristol, that she spectacularly jumped down his staircase in one leap.)

Godwin was successful in having a number of his designs accepted—Northampton Town Hall being probably his most substantial single surviving work. He won the Northampton competition with a revolutionary simple design in an age famous for its love of fussy decoration. After his wife's death in the May of 1864, Godwin opened his own office in London and spent an increasing amount of time there. His main problem was his inability to manage his financial affairs, often getting into debt by sheer mismanagement.

Ellen had admired him from Bristol days and he would be bound to impress and fascinate the impetuous 21 year old. Sympathetic, amusing, sharing her interests, Godwin was the very antithesis of Watts. Yet for Godwin to suggest or agree to eloping, surely aware that this would ruin Ellen's reputation, seems a surprisingly selfish move. Men may have flouted the strict rules of Victorian social behaviour, but women could not. Ellen was a very beautiful young woman: like her, he must have allowed his heart to rule his head.

Ellen counted the next few years as among the happiest of her life. Godwin was to be her enduring love. 'I have the simplest faith that absolute devotion to another human being means the greatest happiness,' she said. 'That happiness was now mine.'[2] She admitted joyfully that she led a most unconventional life and loved living in the country. The view of the grandson of her future stage partner, Henry Irving, was that 'humiliated and frustrated by the mockery of her marriage to Watts' she was 'longing only for the fulfilment of her womanhood in a domestic life'[3].

Her daughter Edy and Chris St John, the co-editors of Ellen's memoirs, preferred to present her as a single-minded artist and not a girl well lost for love. They argued she may not have left the stage voluntarily, but that retirement may have been forced on her. They cite the possible indiscretion with Godwin during her marriage; the disapproval of friends who had promoted her acting career; and her wish not to embarrass her family.

Whatever the reason, Ellen discovered herself, maturing into the unique, self-reliant woman she became. Her friend, the writer Graham Robertson, queried why she was so less stagey and artificial than other actresses, answering his own question by saying: 'I think it was because at the most critical and receptive age of 19, when most young players are working up towards their first success and living wholly in the world behind the footlights, she left the stage and gave what would be considered her best years to a real life, away in the country, far from theatres and all concerning them.'[4]

Ellen delighted in her new life. She began gardening and attempted, haphazardly, to cook. Rising at 6 am, she fed their 200 ducks and chickens. Sometimes she drove out in the pony cart, or would walk across the common to fetch the milk. It was, as she said, 'truly the simple life we led in Hertfordshire. From scrubbing floors and lighting fires, cooking, gardening, and harnessing the pony, I grew thinner than ever—as thin as a whipping-post, a hurdle, or a haddock!'[5] Ellen's son remembered his father buying Ellen a bulldog to protect her in his absence, 'then a parrot was added to the company, then a goat and, finally, a little monkey that liked to perch upon her foot when she sat by the fire at night . . . her leg would go numb, but she hated to wake him!'[6]

Godwin remained charmed by his golden goddess. With their mutual passion for Shakespeare they spent their evenings together reading excerpts from his plays, discussing them and the different ways of presenting them. Godwin loved playing the organ and bought one, and he and Ellen would play Bach's *Prelude and Fugue* late into the night. They also planned the new house which Godwin intended to build for them in Harpenden. He sketched out his ideas for the design of the house and its furniture, interspersed with sketching Ellen, while Ellen planned the garden.

In order to be with Ellen as much as possible, Godwin often worked at home. Ellen contentedly spent her evenings reading to him while he drew, transcribing his notes or tracing his

Ellen had successfully returned to the stage after separating from Watts,
but again gave up acting for a life in the country with Edward Godwin.

elaborate architectural drawings for which she would be paid a
guinea. She worked with him, for example, on The Archeology
of Shakespeare's Plays. One of the few of Godwin's friends who
knew about the hideaway was his fellow architect William Burges

and when he came to stay while Godwin was designing Cardiff Castle's tower, he found Ellen tracing all the room decorations. It was detailed work and Ellen later attributed her poor eyesight to the strain of it, though she also thought it could be due to years of acting by gaslight.

At the time, Godwin was currently designing two large houses in Ireland and when he had to check on the progress of one of these, Dromore Castle, Ellen went with him, impressed by his knowledge of Celtic art, admiring his design for an armchair of oiled wainscot oak and leather and his wall decoration with its Japanese influence.

Godwin's work was becoming in demand. He accepted more professional commitments and found it increasingly hard to remain for long at the cottage. He was now a Fellow of the Royal Institute of British Architects, a Fellow of the Society of Antiquariens and an active member of the Archeological Association whose meetings were often held in Weymouth. Ellen saw less and less of him and it was a decidedly difficult time for her. Because so few knew that she was living with Godwin, and her family, who did, refused to see her, the couple had practically no visitors. There was no one to alleviate her loneliness. With no telephone Godwin was unable to let her know from London or elsewhere that he would be late, or not even returning that night.

Ellen was unaware that her lack of organisation and domesticity was contributing to Godwin's increasing absences. Her view of the country was essentially romantic, but if you intend to drift around romantically, you need servants. Ellen was untidy, unpunctual and extravagant. Marguerite Steen, the biographer of the Terry family, commented that she 'cooked abominable meals for her lover, invariably forgetting some essential ingredient, or letting the dish burn while she petted the animals, or wandered along the hedgerows, gathering autumn leaves and berries, which she was idly arranging while Godwin craved for his supper.'

She commented critically that Godwin was also wholly self-centred and 'took it for granted that his young, beautiful and gifted companion would devote herself to his interests, be grateful for the favours he bestowed (at his convenience) upon her, and act round the clock as his housekeeper, cook, amanuensis, and partner of his bed. He never recognised the crying need in Nelly (Ellen), after her disastrous marriage, of tenderness and care. Of both he was incapable. He was, according to his lights, "in love" with her; but love, to Godwin, carried none of the connotations it implied to a romantic and sensitive girl. A monumental egoist, taking feminine adulation for granted, his increasing professional prestige gradually took precedence of his attachment to Nelly.'[7] Ellen's own romanticised view of the country was dented after some unfortunate incidents. Graham Robertson recalled her telling him 'that on one dismal evening, everything had looked unusually black. She had been alone for many days, funds were very low, she was ill and anxious.' Harnessing the pony, she had driven to meet the last train, hoping that Godwin would be on it 'and put an end to the fears and the loneliness.'

He was, as usual, not on it, and she drove back alone through the dark lanes. Deciding she would not bother to have supper, she took the pony into its stall and gave it some hay. As she was doing so, a mouse fell straight down her back. It was the final straw, said Robertson, 'the darkest hour of her life.'[8]

On another occasion, again returning alone from the station, her lamp went out, leaving her in the pitch dark. 'In a lonely lane a man's rough voice suddenly called out some trivial question. She answered shortly, heard the voice mutter, "My God, it's a gal!" and the next minute a man had sprung into the cart beside her—she felt his hot, whisky-laden breath on her cheek.'[9] Ellen smartly disposed of him by cracking down the whip handle on his head. But this, along with another occasion when she spent a night in a wood rather than squelch through a thick circle of surrounding frogs, contributed to her depression. She was expecting her first child by now and was in a particularly susceptible state.

Inevitably Godwin was away when Ellen gave birth for the first time in 1869. The baby, a girl, was delivered by a Dr Rumball (after his death his wife, Mrs Rumball, became Ellen's devoted companion housekeeper for some 30 years). Years later Ellen was to tell Bernard Shaw that she 'forgot my pangs whilst reading *The Watching of the Falcon* on a certain bitter-sweet night in December when Edy, my first child, was born. They were playing in the church, *O Rest in the Lord*. I heard them as I passed through the

Mrs Rumball, above, was the wife of the country doctor who delivered Ellen's first child, a daughter called Edith. On her husband's death, Mrs Rumball became Ellen's devoted companion-housekeeper for some 30 years and was affectionately known as 'Boo'.

village—alone—feeling frightfully ill and afraid. I could never forget that music and that poem. It was all lovely and awful.'[10] It was a striking contrast to the birth of her sister Kate's second child, born the same year, for Kate was surrounded by a roomful of doctors and nurses, along with a devoted husband and a caring mother to give her all the support she needed.

Ellen's daughter was named Edith after Eadgyth, the daughter of Godwin, Earl of the West Saxons, whom Godwin, archaeologist as well as architect, thought was his likely ancestor. Godwin was again absent when, some two years later on 16th January 1872, Ellen's second child, Teddy, was born and she stayed the night with the midwife. She was delighted to have a son who, because of his light weight, she called 'The feather of England.' Godwin lightheartedly registered Teddy's birth as being the son of 'Eleanor Alice Godwin, formerly Watkins.' It was reminiscent of one of the letters Ellen wrote after the breakup of her marriage to her friend, Mary Ann Hall, in which she signed herself 'Eleanor Alicia Watson'—my new name.'

At the time, Godwin was overseeing their new house at Fallows Green near Harpenden, a house he had promised Ellen to design and build after their original cottage became too small for the growing family. He had kept Ellen aware of its progress, writing affectionately to her the night before the house was ready for occupation to say:

'I have been obliged to have Japan paper curtains for the dining room, the mule cloth wouldn't do, but I've got my own design—lucky, eh?...I think you'll like the 2nd floor, our bedroom dressing room and Lady's Snuggery—the latter I shall leave pretty much for you to dress and do what you like with...We shall not I fear have the curtains ready, but there are blinds and shutters and as it is summer I spose you won't mind more than I do—I have tried hard to push on so as to get one sitting room and one bedroom finished and comfy for us but the weather and other things have conspired against us and I may not be able to do it, so don't grumble more than you can help—you see I live in mortal fear of you, don't I.'[11]

Middle-class parents in Victorian times were normally not too involved with their children—Kate, Ellen's sister, for example, a careful housekeeper who allotted her daily timetable carefully, allowed an hour in conference with the cook, an hour for needlework, an hour playing the piano, an hour to rest and an hour with her baby. Ellen's two children, on the other hand, were her main companions and were outrageously spoilt, as in her eyes they could do no wrong.

They were thrown back on their own resources for entertainment, banned from seeing their cousins, Kate's children.

Ellen recalled this time in later years when writing to her son after his first child had been born: 'When you were helpless I was your servant—I had no servants for you—and I cooked and baked, and washed and sewed for you—and scrubbed for you, and fainted for you, and got well again for you, as my mother did for me.'[12]

Godwin was also more involved with his children than the usual distant Victorian father, having strong ideas on how they should be raised. The nursery wall was hung with Japanese prints and the children were brought up on Walter Crane's prints and picture books. If friends gave the children 'inappropriate' gifts, these were promptly burned. Only simple toys made of wood were acceptable.

So deeply did this philosophy enter the children's minds that on one occasion when Edy, as a tiny child, was given a doll clad in a violent pink dress, she disdainfully spurned it with the damning word, 'Vulgar', then smashed it to pieces, hating its 'pink cheeks, horrid smile and blue ear-rings.' Dolls brought out the worst in her. On another occasion, taken to Madame Tussauds, she fingered the clothes of the waxen Princess of Wales and said, 'Only a disgusting doll.' The painter Whistler, in a politically correct move, gave the children two tiny kimonos to wear. Ellen herself usually wore a kimono.

The two children, who referred to themselves individually as 'Miss Edy' and 'Master Edward' were very different. Teddy, a smiling, fat child, had inherited his mother's charm from the first, and it was to cause the downfall of a large number of women. Edy was more managing and dictatorial, given to hitting Teddy on the head with a wooden spoon. Her brother explained this by saying of his mother that she 'had the idea that women were much too soft and gentle, and men rather too hard and rough. So she set out to keep me soft and gentle and to see that my sister Edy was hard as nails.'[13]

He remembered, one winter, her bringing in two handfuls of snow and banging them on his face with the remark 'There!', though he accepted it was not because she was jealous of his arrival, just generous with her snow. Once, when he admitted to being afraid of the dark, Edy scornfully exhorted him to pull himself together and 'be a woman.' On another occasion, when taken to a circus, Edy was horrified to see the clown apparently fall from the tightrope and chastised her mother, saying 'Take me away! take me away! you ought never to have brought me here.' Teddy could be equally arbitrary, shouting out in the station at a departing train 'Stop the train! I'm Ellen Terry's little boy.'

Ellen adored them both, feeling that she could forgive them anything. Teddy in turn admitted he was born loving his mother: 'she was so spoiling.'

The Harpenden house, its internal decoration and the specially designed furniture had cost a great deal, and there was little enough money to pay the piled-up earlier bills. Ellen was not a careful housekeeper and, to make matters worse, Godwin was involved in a long-running dispute with his former partner, Crisp. Despite their financial position spiralling out of control, Godwin took Ellen and Edy—Teddy being too young—to Normandy, where he wanted to see the Bayeux Tapestry as part of his obsessive research into his antecedents. He also wanted to study Gothic architecture as his public designs were still in that tradition, despite his own preference for a simpler style. His liking for oriental designs forged his friendship with Whistler, who was similarly interested.

Godwin made meticulous sketches during visits to towns like Lisieux and Nantes, examining furnishings and fabrics in chateaux so that he could later incorporate these in his own designs. He had now branched out into designing furnishings and wallpaper in a style reminiscent of William Morris, with oriental motifs of birds and bamboo.

The three of them listened to choirs in churches and cathedrals. When Ellen turned to speak to Edy, who had never heard choirboys singing before, she never forgot the child saying, 'Ssh! ssh! Miss Edy has seen the angels.' It was a memorable family holiday for them: the last they were to enjoy together.

On their return from France in 1873, debts overwhelmed them despite Godwin's commission to design Sunderland's town hall. As Steen observed, Godwin's mind 'was too loftily occupied with the medieval to attend to such mundane trifles as settling bills or keeping up the mortgage payments, the bailiff's men moved in on Fallows End.'[14] Ellen did not help as she inevitably spent the money Godwin gave her not on food but on trinkets or presents for the children or clothes for Mrs Rumball. She rarely spent it on herself: Ellen was generous to a fault with her money all her life.

In the winter of 1873–4 the bailiffs were threatening to remove all the furniture from the mortgaged house. Their finances had moved into an irretrievably dangerous state. Godwin was now 40 and Ellen, 27 herself, could see their long-term relationship was disintegrating. Godwin was rarely home any more and she had finally become disillusioned by his neglect of her and her life in Harpenden.

She poured all her affection into her children, trying to act as both father and mother to them. Although Teddy was to say that 'the blessed lady, my mother, no more knew how to bring up a boy than she knew how to swim', Edy's sharp comment was that she wondered whether 'the problem of bringing up this particular boy, whose character was indeterminate in his abnormally prolonged chrysalis days, would have been tackled more successfully by a father.'[15] The relationship of the brother and sister was constantly edgy.

Who can tell what would have happened? But at that point melodrama took over. Ellen was driving the children in a pony cart when a wheel came off. She was standing in the lane, wondering what to do, when some riders to the hunt jumped over a nearby fence. 'One of them stopped and asked if he could do anything. Then he looked hard at me and exclaimed: "Good God! it's Nelly!"'

The rider was Charles Reade, playwright and old friend of Ellen's…as a child she regarded him as a quasi-father, even laughingly writing to him as 'dear Papa.' He hadn't seen her for years and promptly told her it was time she came back to the stage. She equally promptly refused then, as she recalled later, 'Suddenly I remembered the bailiff in the house a few miles away and I said laughingly: "Well, perhaps I would think of it if some one would give me 40 pounds a week!"'[16]

This was a vast amount of money in those days but to Ellen's surprise Charles Reade immediately accepted her offer. He was just about to stage a play of his, *The Wandering Heir*, based on the Tichbourne Case, at the Queen's Theatre, ironically the same one

Teddy, Ellen's second child, was born in 1872. His mother absolutely adored him, a victim to his straw-coloured hair and angelic smile.

from which Ellen had fled to live with Godwin. Mrs John Wood, who had played the heroine Philippa Chester in its provincial tour, had left for another engagement and Reade, desperate for a replacement, considered Ellen ideal.

Ellen did not want to return to the theatre, but she was hard–headed enough to know that she and Godwin could not continue their present Micawber-style life and bring up the children without a more settled income. More money would enable them to redeem their Harpenden furniture and clear their debts. Godwin was pleased, aware how often he had left Ellen alone while away on projects, and both were conscious that Edy was nearly of school age and London would provide better tuition than the country.

Her son said later that despite his mother's protests at leaving the country, the Terry family always put work first; but he was angry with Reade for promising Ellen £40 a week in salary—a sum he could not guarantee she would continue to earn. To set up house in London without financial security could, and did, only lead to yet more debts. But at the time, the future looked sunny.

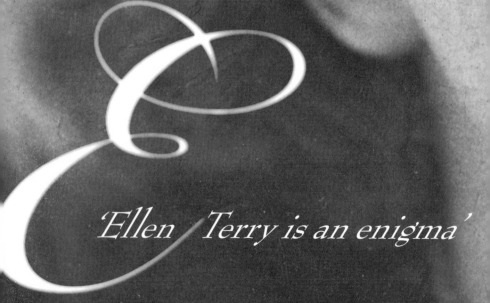

Ellen returned to the stage solely to earn
enough money to keep the bailiffs from
the family door, but her relationship with
Godwin continued to deteriorate. After he left
her, Ellen married the actor Charles Kelly.
At the same time, her acting career began a
meteoric rise.

'Ellen Terry is an enigma'

'Ellen Terry is an enigma. Her eyes are pale, her nose rather long, her mouth nothing particular. Yet somehow she is beautiful'—Charles Reade.

H.S. Mendelss

'Ellen Terry is an enigma'

Ellen's reappearance on the stage in *The Wandering Heir*, which took place on 28th February 1874, was billed as the return of an actress 'after a long period of retirement.' On finding who it was, the audience was highly delighted. Ellen was amazed at the acclamation with which she was welcomed back. The papers were more flattering than they had ever been before, *The Daily Telegraph* critic praising the 'undiminished brightness and buoyancy of her style.'

A reception like this caused Ellen to feel far more enthusiastic about her return to acting this time around than she had on her comeback after her marriage to Watts had failed. Friends she thought would have been estranged by her long absence warmly welcomed her back. *The Wandering Heir* as a play, however, received faint praise. Godwin himself in *The British Architect* admitted it would be wearying to watch 'even if every actor in it were equal to Miss Terry.'

In April Reade cast Ellen in a rather feeble melodrama of his called *It's Never too late to Mend* and after that Ellen toured the provinces with him in several of his plays. She was now re-established as a popular actress, Reade having played an important part in this. He was a mediocre playwright but as Ellen's manager he was first class, watching her progress carefully. During the run of *The Wandering Heir* he sat in a private box every night and sent her notes between acts about the highs and lows of her performance.

Ellen, after such a long absence from the stage, was grateful

69

for advice on improving her acting. Yet although Reade called her 'Eleanora Delicia' as an affectionate variation of her real name, Ellen Alicia, his remarks were pungent: 'I prefer you for my Philippa to any other actress, and shall do so still, even if you will not, or cannot, throw more vigour into the lines that need it,' he said, criticising her for 'limp exits rather than ardent exits.'[1] Ellen realised that after six years off stage her breathing was not under control, explaining her 'limpness.' Reade also taught her the value of moving off the stage with a swift rush.

Nicknaming Ellen his 'artful toad', yet admitting she was 'highly gifted with what Voltaire justly calls *le grand art de plaire*', Reade wrote his impressions of her in his notebook:

'Ellen Terry is an enigma. Her eyes are pale, her nose rather long, her mouth nothing particular. Complexion a delicate brick dust, her hair rather like tow. Yet somehow she is beautiful. Her expression kills any pretty face you see beside her. Her figure is lean and bony, her hand masculine in size and form. Yet she is a pattern of fawn-like grace. Whether in movement or repose, grace pervades the hussy. In character impulsive, intelligent, weak, hysterical—in short all that is abominable and charming in woman…I see through and through her. Yet she pleases me all the same. Little duck![2]

He was also to say of her: 'Soft and yielding on the surface, egotistical below…always wanting something "dreadful bad" today, which she does not want tomorrow, especially if you are weak enough to give it her, or get it her…hard as a nail in money matters, but velvet on the surface. A creature born to please and to deceive.' He added, at a later date, that he had written this while she was 'under the influence of a blackguard and was now greatly improved. The hardness below is melting away.' He called her 'downright fascinating'.[3]

Initially the couple's two children remained in the country. However, Godwin rented a house for them all at 20 Taviton Street, near King's Cross. This made the journey to their house in Harpenden, which they could now afford to keep on, relatively easy. While Ellen was rehearsing and London's peasouper fogs prevailed, the children stayed in Harpenden with their nursemaid, but in the winter of 1874 they joined their parents in London. It was a household of six: Ellen and the children, Godwin, Mrs Rumball (Ellen's companion housekeeper, known as Boo) and her niece, Bo. The actor Johnston Forbes-Robertson, who thought Ellen's performance as Philippa was the absolute spirit of high comedy, went to visit her there and was shown into the drawing room.

He noticed the floor 'was covered with straw-coloured matting, and there was a dado of the same material. Above the dado were white walls, and the hangings were of cretonne, with a fine Japanese pattern in delicate grey-blue. The chairs were of wicker with cushions like the hangings, and in the centre of the room was a full-sized cast of the Venus of Milo, before which was a small pedestal, holding a little censer from which rose, curling round the Venus, ribbons of blue smoke.'

But it was Ellen who drew his real admiration. 'The door opened, and in floated a vision of loveliness! In a blue kimono and with that wonderful golden hair, she seemed to melt into the surroundings and appeared almost intangible.' He was afterwards shown the children: Teddy, still in his cradle, and Edy 'a lively little girl, black-haired, with great inquiring eyes.'[4]

Ellen found that touring with Reade, who had written a one-act play, *Rachael the Reaper*, as a warm-up to *The Wandering Heir* was far from dull. Passionate about realism on stage, he invested in real animals for this countryside play. To Ellen's amazement, 'he began by buying real pigs, real sheep, a real goat, and a real dog. Real litter was strewn all over the stage, much to the inconvenience of the unreal farm-labourer, Charles Kelly, who could not compete with it.'[5] She never forgot Charles Reade's arrival at the theatre in a four-wheeler with a goat and a lot of little pigs, which promptly vanished in all directions. Kelly, who was watching, was greatly relieved to see it. 'I shan't have those damned pigs to spoil my acting as well as the damned dog and the damned goat!' On the first night, the real dog bit Kelly's real ankles, which resulted in him kicking it into the orchestral drum.

Godwin, busy at the time writing a series of 33 articles on the *Architecture and Costume of Shakespeare's Plays*, was asked by Emily Faithful, editor of *Women and Work* and promoter of women's emancipation, to write an article on women's prospects as architects.

Godwin was a great supporter of this idea, considering women had 'that equipoise which is indispensable for the creation of beauty.' The other male members of the profession profoundly disagreed with these views but to underline his seriousness (or perhaps to spite them) he took on a young woman pupil, Beatrice Phillips, the schoolgirl daughter of John Bernie Phillips, the sculptor who executed the frieze on the podium of the Albert Memorial.

Godwin's own interests had slowly changed. He was increasingly involved with the Arts Club where members like Whistler shared his own views on artistic design, which were decidedly out of step with conventional attitudes. His views on Japanese art, a flow of articles in *The Building News* and *The Architect* and his designs for houses for those of moderate means, preoccupied his life. He had no time or interest in being a conventional husband or father and backed away from the financial responsibility.

After the tour, Ellen had no work and began to wonder if she had merely exchanged poverty in the country for poverty in town. Her children were her main concern as her trust in Godwin to look after the family's finances was shattered. She felt the financial responsibility was hers, particularly when Godwin, to avoid the creditors, went to stay with a friend in the Isle of Wight, telling Ellen to 'detain' all the unpleasant letters. When yet again the bailiff's men moved in, she sent the children back to the Harpenden house. It was fortunate Forbes-Robertson chose to visit when he did: after the bailiff's men left, all there was to see was the Venus de Milo statue and the straw matting.

Ellen was extraordinarily fortunate: at certain times in her life when she was financially desperate, a good fairy would turn up in an almost pantomimic way. In this case, the fairy was in the shape of Mrs Marie Bancroft who, together with her husband Squire Bancroft, managed the Prince of Wales Theatre. The two had made it the most fashionable theatre in London by staging domestic comedies (known as the cup-and-saucer dramas).

They decided in 1875 to have a complete change and stage a Shakespearean revival. Their first choice was *The Merchant of Venice* and Mrs Bancroft, elegant in Parisian black, came to ask Ellen to act Portia. It was a gamble on the part of the Bancrofts: Ellen was not known as a Shakespearean actress, having appeared

72

Ellen returned to the stage after country life proved financially disastrous. Mrs Bancroft (above), the former actress Marie Wilton and now part of the Bancroft management, rescued her career when she offered her the part of Portia.

only once as Desdemona and a few times as Katharine the Shrew. On the other hand, as a student of Shakespeare, she already knew the part by heart.

For Ellen, it was a miracle. Saddened by the way the house had been dismantled of some of its most beautiful treasures by the brokers, she admitted that: 'At this time I was very miserable. I was worried to death by domestic troubles and financial difficulties. The house in which I first lived in London, after I left Hertfordshire, had been stripped of some of its most beautiful treasures by the brokers. Pressure was being put on me by well-meaning friends to leave this house and make a great change in my life. Everything was at its darkest when Mrs Bancroft came to call on me.'

She realised how strange she must have looked to her visitor. 'I wore a dress of some deep yellow woollen material which my little daughter used to call the "frog dress" because it was speckled with brown like a frog's skin. It was cut like a Viollet-le-Duc tabard, and had not a trace of the fashion of the time.'[6] Fortunately, Mrs Bancroft was not deterred by her aesthetic dress or her painful thinness.

Ellen's friends like Tom Taylor and Charles Reade were again putting pressure on her to leave Godwin, who was considered by them to be a financial and emotional liability. However, the *Merchant of Venice* changed all that as Mrs Bancroft additionally turned to Godwin for 'archeological help' on the stage design. Ellen was overjoyed: their mutual love of Shakespeare would surely heal any rift and the joint wages would finally keep the bailiffs away. She wrote to Godwin to tell him the good news and he returned from the Isle of Wight and arranged for the children to come back to London from Hertfordshire.

Busy though she was, Ellen had no worries about leaving the children to their own devices. They were both independent and used to amusing themselves. 'I have often thanked heaven,' she said, 'that with all their faults, my boy and girl have never been lazy, and never felt dull. At this time Teddy always had a pencil in his hand, when he wasn't looking for his biscuit—he was a greedy little thing!—and Edy was hammering clothes on to her dolls with tin–tacks! Teddy said poetry beautifully, and when he and his sister were still tiny mites, they used to go through scene after scene of *As You Like It* for their own amusement.'[7] Teddy recalled being walked round London's stony streets at the age of three, along with Edy, who was a good walker. 'I hated dragging along these pavements—besides five year old Edy was strong-minded! I was decidedly not.'

Ellen was to keep all Edy's and Teddy's drawings: careful

paintings of flowers, illustrations of classics and nursery rhymes. On the back of one done by Teddy, Godwin had written to her: 'I'm quite proud of this! No I don't mean that—but—it isn't bad, is it?' Edy signed a painting of hers of an old thatched house 'Edith Terry' and wrote 'Dedicated to dear Mumy'.[8]

The Merchant of Venice opened at the Prince of Wales Theatre on April 15th 1875. Ellen was to say that though she had had success before as an actress that 'Never until I appeared as Portia at the Prince of Wales's had I experienced that awe-struck feeling which comes, I suppose, to no actress more than once in a life-time—the feeling of the conqueror. In homely parlance, I knew that I had "got them" at the moment when I spoke the speech beginning, "You see me, Lord Bassanio, where I stand." "What can this be?" I thought. "Quite this thing has never come to me before! This is different!"'[9]

Godwin had supplied sketches for six out of 21 scenes. He ensured that the scene painters remembered that in 1590 Venice was not a city of palaces or ruins but of three great styles of art, Byzantine, Gothic and the Renaissance and the result was that the sets looked magically like Italian paintings. Out of the hundreds of little sketches in his preserved sketchbooks is his plan of the famous *Merchant of Venice* street scene. The production was so visually beautiful that critics actually protested against it, claiming that the only beauty proper to a Shakespearean performance was the beauty of the spoken word.

Ellen, ethereal in an almond blossom dress, was a triumph as Portia. It was, as Squire Bancroft was to say, the foundation-stone of her mature career. Alice Comyns Carr, who was later Ellen's stage dress designer, remembered that on the first night, when 'the curtain rose upon Nell's tall and slender figure in a china blue and white brocaded dress, with one crimson rose at her breast, the whole house burst forth in rapturous applause. But her greatest effect was when she walked into the court in her black robes of justice, and I remember my young husband, who had rushed out between the acts to buy the last bouquet in Covent Garden, throwing his floral tribute at her feet amidst the enthusiasm of the audience.'[10]

Graham Robertson considered that Ellen was 'the painter's actress' and appealed to the eye before the ear, 'her gestures and pose being eloquence itself; her charm held every one but I think

75

pre-eminently those who loved pictures.'[11]

Ellen was elated and the reviews for her performance of Portia were highly enthusiastic. *The Daily Telegraph* stated that 'Miss Terry, in her beautiful robes, looked as if she had stepped out of a canvas by Mr Leighton. She took us back to old Venice quite as much as Mr Godwin's "archeological research".' It considered the comedy scenes in which she took part as very perfect acting, in the style of art which cannot be taught.' *The Daily News* praised her bold innocence, lively wit and quick intelligence, along with her grace and elegance of manner and depth of passion, and considered her performance essentially artistic.

Ellen was unlucky in one rather crucial regard: the actor who played Shylock, Charles Coghlan, gave an extremely poor performance and the Bancrofts openly admitted that as the play had failed to attract large audiences, it would be withdrawn after three weeks. Ellen was to say 'Short as the run of the play was, it was a wonderful time for me. Everyone seemed to be in love with me! I had sweethearts by the dozen, known and unknown. Most of the letters written to me I destroyed long ago, but the feeling of sweetness and light with which some of them filled me can never be destroyed.'[12]

The Bancrofts were also delighted with Ellen's performance, but had no immediate play in mind to stage after the withdrawal of *The Merchant of Venice*. In the March of 1877 they finally cast Ellen as Clara Douglas in *Money*, an old-fashioned comedy by Lord Lytton. She enjoyed playing the rational Clara though Tom Taylor had no hesitation in writing to her to criticise her acting, saying: 'But you were nervous and uncomfortable in many parts for want of sufficient rehearsal...I would only urge on you the great importance of studying to be quiet and composed, and not fidgeting. There was especially a trick of constantly twiddling with and looking at your fingers which you should, above all, be on your guard against.'[13]

Ellen, used to criticism from Charles Reade, was in no way cast down by Tom Taylor's comments: she was always remarkably modest and eager to learn. Tom Taylor acted as another quasi-father. In talking about her own father she said dispassionately that he 'was charming, but Irish and irresponsible. It was not in his temperament to give wise advice and counsel.'

Ellen herself was quick to promote other actors if she could. Indeed, she wrote to the Bancrofts to say 'Have you ever seen Mr Kelly act?…He can show gradation of feeling—and has the tenderest voice I've ever heard.'[14]

While with the Bancrofts, Ellen was offered the parts of Juliet and Rosalind by Charles Calvert, the manager of the Prince's Theatre in Manchester. The offer came to nothing, but Godwin had already planned her wardrobe for Juliet, writing to tell her that one of his designs for her, a square mantle of fluffy transparent eastern stuff about six feet six inches square, 'worn anyhow, but your how especially.' He wrote again on 24th July from the Verulam Club, in St James Street, in a letter illustrated by a detailed drawing of Juliet's scent bottle to say:

'Darlin–one word–you took away all memory, thought, archaeology and the rest today. Of course you can have silk for Juliet–pale red–pale blue–violet and a kind of vermillion were used mostly in 1300–10. Swell dresses like her ball dress may be embroidered all over…but then you might be happier if you were Juliet from top to toe. I can't trust myself to write two words apart from what you call "business." You will believe this and credit me with something human.'[15]

Why did he emphasise the need to be thought human? And why the letter from the club? Despite the affection at the start of this letter, the truth was that only a month before *The Merchant of Venice* was due to start, in the April of 1875, Edward had left Ellen.

Their son, Teddy, could only guess at the reason that Godwin had left Taviton Street, apparently in a towering rage, never to return. 'Was he piqued at playing such a secondary part in a theatre where Ellen was so obviously the professional while he was the amateur? Did he resent the attention paid to her by other male members of the company…or did Ellen remark upon the amount of attention he was paying to his assistant, Beatrice Phillips?' Commenting that they parted 'by mutual disagreement' he added 'Sad: but there was no unkindness, no dissension—they were neither of them desertable people.'[16]

Ellen's daughter Edy, in her notes to her mother's memoirs, wrote that she too was later told by an old friend of Godwin's that he had left Taviton Street 'in a fit of pique.' But although there were a number of reasons why Godwin had fallen out with Ellen, as she was no demure milk-and-water mistress and must have been a demanding companion, the seven-year relationship must have worn very thin if they were unable to patch up a fit of pique.

Poverty has to have played a part in snapping the strands of the relationship: Ellen's friends were constantly urging her to leave her precarious financial life with Godwin. And living openly with him in London must have attracted more censure than they would have received in the relative privacy of the countryside.

In a letter Ellen wrote to a friend of Harpenden days in 1890, four years after Godwin's death, she still did not clarify the reason for the break, but clearly showed the depth of her feeling for him: 'The times, of which you were part, were my best times, my happiest times...He went away and shut the door after him. It seems like that to me, but he knows.'[17]

After Godwin left, Ellen and her household moved to 221 Camden Road. It was more rural, on a hill and had the advantage of a large garden where the children could play.

Ellen's grandson, Edward Craig, came across a letter from Ellen to a Mr Wilson, sent from Camden Road but with a pencilled note on it reading 'before March 6', which throws into question just when the relationship broke up. Matters were obviously more complicated than they appeared on the surface:

'In all gentleness and kindness of feeling, I must beg you not to act as mediator between Mr Godwin and myself. Our separation was a thing agreed upon by both of us many weeks before it actually took place. The first steps were taken by him and I certainly am much astonished to hear that he professes any strong feeling in the matter. Part of our compact was that we should always maintain a kindly, friendly relation to another—He has since Tuesday last made this an IMPOSSIBILITY. He tried by unfair means to get my little girl from me (I had offered to let him have the boy) and I now distinctly refuse to hold any communication whatever with him...

'If Mr Godwin's friends knew his temperament as I do and the effects of change of scene upon him, they would advise his leaving London and staying with friends, for a time at least. He should not go alone as he is apt to brood and imagine all kinds of ills which

Ellen's children, Teddy and Edy, were the focus of her life. Edy, a fiercer character than Teddy, once exhorted her brother, when he admitted to being afraid of the dark, 'to be a woman!'

do not exist. You say in your letter "I really fear for his reason"— When I knew him in his home life 13 years ago I had the same idea, and at that time he had an utterly sorrowless life—a devoted help-mate—success—friends—everything. He never was happy—he never will be...At the risk of being called utterly heartless I again say I will hold no further communication with Mr Godwin, and I also say that this hard behaviour on my part has been brought about entirely by his own rash conduct since the last time we were together in Taviton Street.'[18]

Ellen ended saying she remained sorrowful in spirit though stronger in health and purpose and added that the children were well, apart from colds.

If Ellen's allegation against Godwin is true, it was extra-ordinarily unnecessary and foolish behaviour on his part, behaviour which he must have known would alienate Ellen. It understandably frightened Edy too. Her brother claimed that she hated her father for ever afterwards, saying she had asked him if he would like to see a portrait of my father, whom he had not seen since he was three years old, 'and instantly she whipped out a terrible drawing someone had made for her, of a fiend with long teeth and claws and a tail, and said, "There that's him!"'[19]

Ellen rather nervously sent the two children off to the Norfolk coast in charge of their nursemaid, Bo. At the time, when a woman married her money and property was immediately and legally merged with that of her husband. He could also legally remove the children from his wife should they separate. These rulings, however, did not apply to Godwin as he was not married to Ellen.

The children eventually joined Ellen at the Camden Town lodgings, which were rather cramped. Ellen, however, was still short of money and had to take the bus to and fro from the theatre and deny herself all luxuries. The following year she was able to afford a more permanent residence at 33 Longridge Road, near Earls Court.

Godwin, despite his behaviour, remained the love of Ellen's life and she was distraught and almost unable to function when he left her. Her son said that after the final split in November 1875, 'E.T. worked on. Brave. Strange to realise now that she did not kill herself.'

In the January of 1876, Godwin married his pupil, Beatrice Phillips. Ellen, perhaps to find a peaceful escape outside London, rented a tiny whitewashed cottage in Hampton Court Road. It had four or five rooms and the back windows looked out on to Bushey Park where stags and deers roamed around. Here she and the children could relax and spend their summers.

Ellen recalled the two children running wild there, dressed in blue and white check pinafores, their hair closely cropped. 'They were always ready to show visitors (not so numerous then as now) the sights; prattled freely to them of "my mamma" who was acting in London, and showed them the new trees which they had assisted the gardeners to plant in the wild garden, and christened after my parts. A silver birch was Iolanthe, a maple Portia, an oak Mabel Vane.'[20]

Edy had reacted coolly when Ellen had recently taken the part of Mabel Vane in *Masks and Faces* by Charles Reade and Tom Taylor, telling her: 'You did look long and thin in your grey dress. When you fainted I thought you was going to fall into the orchestra—you was so long.'[21]

The children made friends with the uniformed old soldier who guarded the gates to Richmond Park for, as Teddy said, few could resist his sister Edy who was taller than he was, 'very handsome' and also bolder. He remembered her saying, 'Come along, Teddy, don't be a coward.' The two children also performed *As You Like It* for the Palace custodians.

They were thrown back on themselves for entertainment as Ellen was still not in touch with the rest of the Terry family. Her children had never met their cousins or their grandparents as Ellen remained a disgrace to them: an unmarried mother with two illegitimate children. In Victorian society this was unacceptable.

Her son recalled that at the time their education consisted of 'verses of Blake, picture books of Walter Crane and Caldecott', but that he himself was delighted when lessons on literature and history stopped for lunch, 'All a lovely dream of food.' But these were his last days of home education.[22]

At Longridge Road, the family's neighbours were Walter Sickert and Sir Edwin Arnold. Their children attended a school run by a Mrs Cole and Edy and Teddy joined them. Teddy was now six and found school most exciting. Mrs Cole was very advanced in her attitudes: she was a supporter of the new women's movement and, equally rare for those days, considered that girls ought to have as good an education as boys. She was a pioneer of co-education and took pupils of both sexes. Edy said that when the two of them first went to the school they were the most backward of all the pupils except for drawing, music and Shakespeare.

Ellen was now the sole financial provider—hough in effect she had been that for the last year or so. Her professional life proceeded with a series of rather uneventful parts under the Bancroft management. In all, she stayed a year at the Prince of Wales Theatre with the Bancrofts before moving in 1876 to the Court, under the management of John Hare. The universally excellent reviews she had received when with the Bancrofts had not just re-established her as an actress, but as a rising theatrical star and from now until the end of the century she was rarely out of work.

She also had a charismatic effect on her audiences. The love letters continued to arrive: all her life she was to attract men. But her legendary charm, which brought men to their knees, also affected women. She had a number of close women friends along with a raft of loyal young women followers, many of whom she generously helped in their acting career. She didn't praise indiscriminately, however, saying of one would–be actress, 'It's sad, my dear, she's bound to be disappointed. You can't do what she's trying to unless you can act.'

Ellen opened at the Court in the November of 1876 in a comedy called *Brothers*. She played the heroine, Kate. It was a rather lack-lustre affair, but Ellen was praised in the magazine *The Academy* for bringing 'into high relief all that is good in the dialogue.'

Ironically on 13th March 1877, a year after Godwin's re-marriage, Watts decided to divorce Ellen on the grounds of her adultery with Godwin. He was now more able to afford such an expensive legal move and possibly one of Ellen's friends like Tom Taylor may have approached him to point out that her social position was seriously jeopardised by the Godwin episode, resulting in her children having no surname. It was of no great matter while they lived in Harpenden, but Ellen was now very much centre stage and her private life was becoming public.

Ellen was cast in a number of plays at the Court, none of which really caught the public imagination. One was Tom Taylor's *New Men and Old Acres* (in which she captivated Bernard Shaw) and another, opening 6th October 1877, was the comedy *The House of Darnley* by Lord Lytton, in which Ellen played Lady Julia Darnley and about which she said, 'It was not a good play, and I was not good in it.'

One of the cast was Charles Wardell, whose stage name was Charles Kelly. Ellen had already acted with him in *The Wandering Heir* when Charles Reade memorably brought his collection of animals on stage. In November, according to her son, Ellen and Charles Kelly married, although Ellen herself said it was during the run of her next play, *Olivia*.

By marrying Ellen successfully achieved overnight respectability. She had calling cards printed immediately, with the name Mrs Wardell, and at last her family were willing to receive her, her husband and the two children. She wrote to an old friend in delight at the reconciliation, saying 'Thank God, mother is alive, and I can atone to her for the pain I unintentionally caused her.'

Charles Kelly Wardell was a widower aged 36, with a reputable

After Godwin left Ellen, she married the actor Charles Kelly ('a manly bulldog') in 1878. It brought about a reconciliation with her family and social respectability. She had visiting cards printed with her married name.

background. His father was a Northumberland clergyman and Charles had originally been a soldier, fighting in the Crimean War, before turning to the theatre. He was physically rugged—a type that always attracted Ellen. She said of him that 'Charles, physically a manly bulldog sort of man, possessed as an actor great tenderness and humour.' Edy, who was eight years old at the time, commented

Ellen in 1878, the year when at the Court Theatre she had a great success in the play Olivia, *based on* The Vicar of Wakefield.

dispassionately on the relationship years later that, 'It is conceivable that she was strongly attracted by Charles Wardell. All through her life the man of brains competed for her affections with the man of brawn.' She admitted that Kelly showed a genuine affection towards her and Teddy, but that he turned out to have 'a violent and jealous temper which Ellen Terry eventually found intolerable.'[23]

That, however, was in the future. At the time there was great jubilation at Longridge Road that the children had a new father.

Teddy, in particular, aged five, was tired of the female ménage around him and welcomed a man about the house. He practised writing his new name on everything. His stately, white–haired grandmother (Sarah Terry) now began to visit them and he helped assure her they were respectable once more. Lewis Carroll, too, wrote to Ellen, graciously suggesting they now renew their friendship.

After her marriage, Ellen and her husband went on tour together. Then in March 1878 Ellen was cast at the Court in the main part in *Olivia*, a play by W G Wills, based on *The Vicar of Wakefield*. She was triumphantly successful as the vicar's daughter, giving a spirited performance and charming the public: postcards of her in the role were to flood the country. Ellen led current fashions, with young women sporting ruffled Olivia caps and scarves. Charles Kelly was less enthused, annoyed at not having been offered the leading part of the vicar in *Olivia*. In this play Ellen's two children walked on to the stage for the first time. 'Teddy had such red cheeks that they made all the rouged cheeks look quite pale! Little Edy gave me a bunch of real flowers that she had picked in the country the day before.'[24]

Ellen's success in this play had a lasting effect on her and on the history of the English stage as it led directly to actor-manager Henry Irving's invitation to her to become his leading lady at the Lyceum Theatre, where he was sole lessee. He had not seen her performance as Olivia, but his friend Lady Pollock told him that Ellen would make him an ideal partner.

Ellen found that the 40-year-old Henry Irving who called on her at Longridge Road in 1878 was very different from the Petruchio with whom she had acted ten years previously. He had, she saw, lost much of his stiff self-consciousness and was now a man of the world. Ellen was now also much more experienced: ten years younger than Irving, she had played 84 parts in a stage career of 22 years.

After negotiations, Ellen was engaged as leading lady for the Lyceum for 40 guineas a week. 'I have engaged Ellen Terry—not a bad start—eh?' Irving wrote to his old headmaster, Dr Pinches. Until then, under various managements, Ellen had achieved popular success but no financial security: now for the first time her money worries were over. Within a few days of Irving's announcement of the start of his new regime at the Lyceum, every seat was sold.

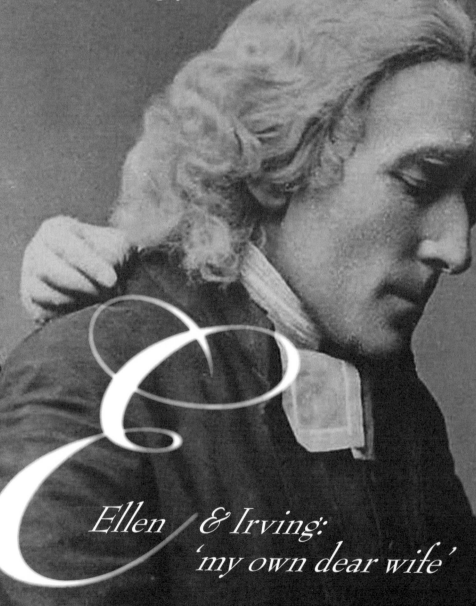

As Henry Irving's leading lady at the Lyceum, Ellen became the foremost actress in Britain. She was to say that 'My chief difficulty in giving a consecutive narrative of my first years at the Lyceum is that Henry Irving looms across them, reducing all events, all feelings, and all that happened, to insignificance'.

Ellen & Irving: 'my own dear wife'

Ellen became Henry Irving's leading lady at the Lyceum Theatre in 1878, aged 31.
Their intense partnership, both personal and professional, lasted over 20 years.

Ellen & Irving: 'my own dear wife'

Both Ellen and Henry Irving had dazzled London on stage, Ellen as Portia and Irving, who had a taste for melodrama, in his haunting performance as Matthias in *The Bells*. In 1878, when Ellen joined Irving at the Lyceum, she was 31 and he was 40. Their stage partnership was to last a quarter of a century.

Ellen had been born into the theatre, but Irving had had a long and difficult 20-year climb to the top. Born in Somerset in 1838—his real name was John Henry Brodribb—he had no theatrical precedent. His father, Samuel Brodribb, was a travelling salesman whose wife, Mary Behenna, was a devout Cornish woman. With little work available in Somerset, his parents moved to London to establish themselves and left four-year-old John Henry with an aunt in Cornwall. He was a lonely and reserved boy, given to reading Shakespeare and the Bible, and retreated from people through play-acting. He once let his emotions show through when he spotted a baby lamb gazing at him through a hedge and went over to kiss it. It bit him.

When he was 11 he joined his parents in London where his father had some minor job, possibly a caretaker. John joined the other 30 pupils at the City Commercial School. Having always since childhood wanted to be an actor, he eagerly looked forward to elocution lessons, excelling in the school's theatrical presentations. More practically, on leaving school at 13, his parents arranged for him to join a business firm as a junior clerk.

However, his old elocution class took over the Soho Theatre

for an evening performance of *Romeo and Juliet*, with Brodribb as Romeo. With the chance of setting foot on the professional stage for the first time, his interest in acting was once again fired. He decided to call himself Henry Irving, choosing the surname Irving because he admired the writer Washington Irving, and paid for playbills which proclaimed 'First Appearance of Mr Irving as Romeo.' His career as an actor started after he was unexpectedly offered a job by the proprietor of the theatre.

Irving spent the next ten wearisome years acting over 600 different roles in provincial theatre companies like Edinburgh and Dublin, rising from 'Walking Gentleman' to Juvenile Lead. He spent some five years in Manchester and made occasional appearances in London, one or two of which were successful. His part as the villain in the play *Hunted Down* by Dion Boucicault, for instance, brought him praise from Clement Scott, the respected critic of the *Sunday Times*, who said Irving was the first actor 'to undermine the artificialities of the old school.' Other admirers included George Eliot and W S Gilbert. Colonel Bateman, who had leased the Lyceum Theatre in 1871, eventually decided to take on Irving as lead actor.

It was his acclaimed performance there as Matthias in the melodrama *The Bells* that galvanised London into awareness of him as an actor. He played an inn-keeper, Matthias, who intercepts a rich customer driving his sledge and murders him for his gold. Years later he hears the bells of the sleigh again, dreams he is discovered and is about to be hanged and chokes to death. His cry of 'the Bells, the Bells' chilled watchers and the critics were ecstatic.

It had, however, one unexpected and serious consequence. Irving, who had married a Florence O'Callaghan on 15th July 1869 and now had two children, was driving back with her after the first-night party after *The Bells*. He said to her with pleasure that they would in future be able to afford their own carriage and pair. Florence, who had a jealous temper and was annoyed at the adulation Henry was receiving, snapped back, 'Are you going on making a fool of yourself like this all your life?'

They were crossing Hyde Park Corner as she spoke and Henry asked the driver of the brougham to stop. 'Without a word he got out and left his wife to continue the journey alone. He never

An image of Henry Irving by the painter William Nicholson. Nicholson's engravings on wood, with their striking simplicity of design, fascinated Ellen's son Ted, who grew increasingly interested in stage design.

returned to his home and he never spoke to her again.'[1] He lived for the next 27 years at a small flat at 15a Grafton Street, usually having dinner with friends at the Garrick Club. With meticulous courtesy he sent his wife tickets for a box at all of his first nights.

Irving came to an amicable arrangement with Mrs Bateman to buy the lease of the Lyceum Theatre from her. He decided to stage *Hamlet* as the first play of the season, to start on 30th December 1878. He had chosen well in taking Ellen as his leading lady. As

Irving's grandson pointed out, 'Under the tutelage of Watts she had learnt to appreciate the rudiments of classical art, and as the working companion of Godwin she had become steeped in the advanced aesthetics of the day. She brought to the Lyceum a well developed sense of colour and design and the critical standards of the world of art beyond the theatre.'[2] Although her own son considered she had only 'a woman's taste' for beautiful things and lacked creative skill as a stage producer, Irving increasingly relied on her judgement over artistic decisions.

As for Ellen, when she looked back at that time she was to say, 'My chief difficulty in giving a consecutive narrative of my first years at the Lyceum is that Henry Irving looms across them, reducing all events, all feelings, all that happened, and all that was suggested, to insignificance.'[3] She admitted that Irving was an egotist 'and all his faults sprang from egotism, which is in one sense, after all, only another name for greatness. So much absorbed was he in his own achievements that he was unable or unwilling to appreciate the achievements of others.'[4]

Ellen's character was a mass of contradictions and complexities. She was nervous about her first appearance at the Lyceum and Irving failed to realise that she needed confidence and guidance from him as to how to play the part of Ophelia.

Irving rehearsed as Hamlet wearing a cloak and carrying a rapier and during the first rehearsal he read everyone's part except Ellen's. Ellen watched him and remembered that 'The power that he put into each part was extraordinary. He threw himself so thoroughly into it that his skin contracted and his eyes shone. His lips grew whiter and whiter, and his skin more and more drawn as time went on, until he looked livid but still beautiful. He then constantly re-rehearsed the first scene on the battlements, in order to get from the actors the intensity required to 'start the play a living thing.'[5]

Irving normally studied the play he intended to stage for some three months before calling the first rehearsal, when he would read every part in the play exactly as he planned it for the first night. While reading, he made notes on the order of the crowds and processions and the position of the characters. He then gave out the written parts to the actors. The next day the cast would meet to 'compare' the parts and check their cues. The initial stand-up rehearsal of the first act under Irving's sole supervision would be three days later and could well last a day; similarly with future acts. There was no lunch interval.

The company soon learned to watch Irving's arrival for rehearsals carefully. If he wore a silk top hat, that meant that he had a later social engagement and would leave after giving them a relatively peaceful day; if, however, he wore a broad-brimmed soft felt hat—which was soon dubbed his 'storm hat'—then they knew they were in for a bad time.

Edwin Booth, after working with Irving, considered he was despotic on stage. 'At rehearsal his will is absolute law, whether it concern the entry of a Messenger with a letter, or the reading of a letter by Miss Terry.'[6] Ellen's son, who liked to control, admired this male power, saying in later years that the so-called partnership between his mother and Irving was no such thing. 'There was only one head of the house, and it was Irving.'

Irving paid meticulous attention to technicalities, like music, duels, crowd scenes and gas lighting cues, but concentrated mainly on the male actors. With only ten days to the opening night he had still not rehearsed his scenes with Ellen. It may have shown the company that he had every trust in her, but she grew anxious and miserable and asked him if they could not rehearse. He merely said to her, 'We shall be all right, but we are not going to run the risk of being bottled up by a gas man or fiddler.' He was concerned that the play wasn't halted by wrong lighting or a misplaced musical cue.

He kept a tight hand on the play, however. Ellen mentioned to him that she intended to wear black for her final 'mad scene.' Irving listened gravely to her, but his dresser came to Ellen later to ask if she were really serious about wearing black. On her asking why not, he said 'Why not? My God! Madam, there must be only one black figure in this play, and that's Hamlet.' Ellen gave way and wore white, realising that Irving had a better sense of scene.

She visited the local 'madhouse' in order to study deranged women so that she could give an authentic performance. She saw one woman laugh, without a gleam of laughter in her face, and a thin, young and pathetic girl gazing at the wall with a vacant face,

Ellen's first part at the Lyceum was Ophelia. *To act the character successfully, she went to a 'madhouse' to study the behaviour of the inmates.*

then suddenly 'she threw up her hands and sped across the room like a swallow. I never forgot it...the movement was as poignant as it was beautiful.'[7]

Ellen found that most of the inmates were, ironically, too theatrical to copy and said that the visit had shown her that it was essential for actors to imagine first and create an image in their mind. Only after that should they observe. Merely reproducing experiences was not enough. She hadn't the advantage of one 17th-century actress called Mrs Mountford who had often played Ophelia but finally became insane. One day, in a lucid interval, she asked what was on at the playhouse and on hearing it was *Hamlet* managed with cunning to elude the attendants and make her way there. She concealed herself until Ophelia entered for the mad scene, then pushed the real actress aside and went on stage, playing the part with perfect representation.

Ellen was unhappy with her own performance as Ophelia.

'When the first night came, I did not play the part well, although the critics and the public were pleased. To myself I failed. I had not rehearsed enough.'[8] Overwrought and believing she had been under-rehearsed, she rushed out of the theatre before curtain call in a cloud of misery, driving up and down the Embankment in a cab before finally going home. Her husband was playing in the aptly named *The Crisis* round the corner at the Haymarket Theatre, but it's not known if they met. Ellen was not reassured until the following day when she found the critics had unanimously praised her performance.

The Times said 'Miss Terry is without a rival' and *Punch* claimed 'Nothing like it has been seen on the English stage in *Punch's* memory.' The critic Charles Hiatt said her whole performance had an infinite pathos: 'Intelligence she always gives us; here she gave us actual inspiration.' Her Ophelia, he said, was not a mad Ophelia but an insane one. She showed 'the terrible spectacle of a normal girl become hopelessly imbecile as the result of overwhelming mental agony...a creature whose mind is so shattered as to be beyond hope or help.'[9] The director of the Theatre Française commented that she looked like the apparition of a Pre-Raphaelite saint while the *Saturday Review* claimed that Ellen was to the English stage what Sarah Bernhardt was to the French stage.

Ellen thought that of all the plays in which Irving acted at the Lyceum, *Hamlet* was his greatest triumph, his acting having an infinite variety. His reviews, however, were good but mixed. He was later to ask Ellen if he thought the 'ill-natured criticism' of his walk was in any way justified and if he really said 'Gud' for 'God.' She was quite honest about it and said that he did indeed drag his leg and say his vowels in a peculiar way.

Irving was not upset: he was always seeking to improve his performance. Ellen was always quick to reassure him, however, and never laughed at his worries. She knew he was so self-conscious about his thin legs that he padded them and said calmly, 'What do you want with fat, pudgy, prizefighter legs!' Irving stopped padding them and also took her advice about relaxing in his dressing room before his entrance rather than standing tensely in the wings, waiting for his cue. On one occasion, when Irving was stumbling over a particular passage, she gave him a list of the words with which he was having difficulty. He studied them and then went on, speaking the passage perfectly.

Ellen also had to cope with Irving's frequent depression. She recalled his melancholy during the *Hamlet* days, in particular, as being appalling. 'I remember feeling as if I had laughed in church,' she said, 'when he came to the foot of the stairs leading to my dressing-room and caught me sliding down the bannisters! He smiled at me, but didn't seem able to get over it.'[10]

Frank Benson, then an actor at the Lyceum, recalled how Ellen in one of her irresponsible moods, caught hold of some scenery that was being hoisted to the flies, hanging on gracefully with strong arms until she was some 40 feet above the stage, whereupon those hauling the scenery suddenly spotted their leading lady and in terror lowered her down gently. They then saw her dance an impromptu Irish jig to show how much better she felt for her aerial flight.[11]

Her quick changes of mood also puzzled Irving: one minute she was laughing with other actors, then she produced tragic tears on stage minutes later. He was unhappy with her unprofessional behaviour when she laughed uncontrollably on stage when anything amused her. On the other hand, he too joined in her laughter when they came across a small girl waiting for her mother. Irving asked what part she was playing. 'Please, sir, first I'm a water-carrier, then I'm a little page, and then I'm a virgin.'

Hamlet ran for 108 nights to a crowded house. Irving's policy for the Lyceum was to show a mixture of Shakespeare, new plays and popular revivals and Ellen was to say that her memory of being at the Lyceum was the sheer work. 'What with acting, rehearsing, and studying—25 reference books were a "simple coming-in" for one part—I sometimes thought I should go blind and mad.'[12]

Her son Teddy remembered at the time that Ellen 'remained in her bedroom until lunch time, sometimes later, unless she had a rehearsal at the theatre—for she would return late at night to the house, tired after her performance of an exhausting part, and might not get to bed until one-thirty or even two.' Her supper would be ready waiting for her, along with her letters, and after eating she would potter around. 'All things had some interest for her—she never idled, but at night she looked at this or at that and gradually drifted upstairs to bed—but not hurriedly: slowly she moved from one room to another and from one interest to another, talking or alone and humming and so off to sleep.'[13]

The second of the Lyceum productions was *The Lady of Lyons* by Lord Lytton. It was adequate, but no more. The critic Clement Scott wrote 'If the Pauline of Miss Ellen Terry is overcharged with fantastic sentiment, the Claude of Mr Irving is overwhelmed with abiding sorrow.' The first night audience, however, welcomed it enthusiastically.

In the June of 1879, the Comedie Francaise visited London with the cast including the eminent Sarah Bernhardt. Both Ellen and Irving grew very attached to her over the years—Ellen called her Sally B–though Ellen considered that Irving never really appreciated Bernhardt's powers as an actress, being too absorbed in his own achievements to allow him to appreciate the achievements of others.

Both Irving and Ellen were dedicated to their profession, yet were remarkably different in temperament. Irving, summed up by his grandson Laurence Irving, was 'single-minded, self-centred and self-sufficient', as opposed to Ellen being essentially extrovert, 'easily distracted, prone to further anyone's interests but her own, and lacking the power of concentration.'[14] But Ellen admired rather than deprecated Irving's egotism and accepted that all his faults sprang from this. He always, she said, put the theatre first. 'He lived in it, he died in it. He had none of my bourgeois qualities—the love of being in love, the love of a home, the dislike of solitude. I have always thought it hard to find my inferiors. He was sure of his high place.'[15]

Ellen's daughter, Edy, was later to counter-argue the idea of Ellen being more woman than artist, pointing out that her work was always the most important factor in her life; that most of her time at home was spent nursing her energy for rehearsals and performances; that her house was managed better by others than herself; and that significantly none of her domestic relationships lasted as long as her 20-year artistic relationship with Irving.[16]

Despite the popularity of The Comedie Française, it failed to lure away the large and enthusiastic audiences at the Lyceum

Theatre. Ellen and her husband were to act a brief reprise of a comedietta called *All is Vanity*, which they had previously done while on tour. It was the only time the couple ever acted together at the Lyceum and was merely a one–off benefit performance. A revived drama by W G Wills, *The Fate of Eugene Aram*, opened on 6th June, with Ellen cast as the heroine, Ruth Meadows. The play gave more acting opportunities to Irving, but in another revival following this, *Charles I*, also by Wills, Ellen shone in the part of Queen Henrietta Maria. Indeed, the first season of the Lyceum turned out to be a major success, making some £7,000 after all expenses including salaries had been paid.

At the end of the season, Irving departed on holiday but Ellen went on a further exhausting provincial tour with her husband. She was well used to hard work and said that the qualities actors needed 'before the art of emotion can make itself felt' were the three I's: 'Imagination, Individuality, and Industry.' She considered that 'Imagination will give the insight required to make an actor one with the character he is assuming; individuality, if sufficiently developed, will enable him to hold any audience; and industry—well, without that no one ever became an artist on the stage or in the studio.'[17]

Their provincial tour started at the Theatre Royal, Birmingham on 18th August, moved to Glasgow in September and then to Liverpool. It was at the Prince of Wales's Theatre in Liverpool that they enacted Charles Reade's adaptation of Tennyson's poem *Dora*. Ellen was worried about whether Reade would approve of their interpretation of the characters, but he wrote to her saying 'Nincompoop! What have you to fear from me for such a masterly performance! Be assured nobody can appreciate your value and Mr Kelly's as I do. It is well played all round.'[18]

Ellen returned to the Lyceum in the late autumn of 1878. Irving then staged a couple of revivals but having spent some of his holiday cruising around the Mediterranean, his thoughts had turned to those of Shakespeare's plays set in Italy. He decided to stage *The Merchant of Venice*, with Ellen as Portia. It opened on 1st November 1879 and theatre-goers were astounded by the lavishly realistic set that had been created for the play.

Such magnificent sets were one of the draws of the Lyceum

Ellen as Portia *in the Lyceum production of* The Merchant of Venice
*in 1879. She received glowing eulogies from the critics, although in
Tennyson's opinion her performance in the trial scene was slightly
wanting in dignity and authority.*

Theatre: few plays until then had been mounted with such attention
to detail. The costumes were based on Italian portraits, the scene
settings recreated from actual buildings.

Ellen occasionally argued with Irving over the interpretation
of her part, and her later lectures on Shakespeare's heroines show
her to have decided views on these, but she was usually willing

to forgo her concept and fit in with Irving's ideas. She said of *The Merchant of Venice* that Irving's Shylock 'necessitated an entire revision of my conception of Portia, especially in the trial scene… I had considered, and still am of the same mind, that Portia in the trial scene ought to be very quiet. I saw an extraordinary effect in this quietness. But as Henry's Shylock was quiet, I had to give it up. His heroic saint was splendid, but it wasn't good for Portia.'[19] It was indeed Irving who produced a more humane, dignified Shylock, a completely different playing of the character from the usual caricature of a mercenary Jewish money-lender.

However, the two actors always managed to complement each other and in her scene with Bassiano Ellen left her quietness behind and showed an unusual forthrightness and ardour.

Some of the reviewers considered her concept of Portia to be excellent. One critic said that to him, 'the essential womanhood of the character was, for the first time in the modern theatre, adequately interpreted and conveyed.'[20] Others were less impressed. Ruskin thought that Irving should have taught her 'a grander reading' of the part and an anonymous critic in *Blackwood's Magazine* considered Ellen turned Portia 'to favour and to prettiness', but did not attempt to produce the distinction and dignity the part deserved. Held up for particular criticism was her scene with Bassiano, particularly her 'coming-on disposition' in her bearing towards her lover. Henry James was equally critical of the scene, writing that Ellen 'giggles too much, plays too much with her fingers, is too free and familiar, too osculatory, in her relations with Bassanio.'[21]

Most critics, however, extravagantly praised her performance, using descriptions like 'infinite pathos', 'picturesque, tender, and womanly throughout', and 'wonderful charm.' Ellen reacted spiritedly on reading these critics saying, 'There is something more in my acting than charm.'

Irving received mixed reviews. Graham Robertson considered that Irving's heroic aristocratic martyr upset the balance of the play and ruined Portia's Trial Scene. 'How small and mean sounded her quibbling tricky speeches when addressed to a being who united the soul of Savonarola and the bearing of Charles I with just a touch of Lord Beaconsfield that made for mystery.'[22]

What the arguments in the many reviews showed was how seriously the Shakespeare plays at the Lyceum were being taken. It was Irving's consuming wish that the theatre should gain respectability and be regarded seriously and he was clearly on his way to achieving this. Before opening with *Hamlet* he had spent £4,000 on transforming the Lyceum. The faded auditorium was repainted in sage green and turquoise blue; the seats in the stalls and dress circle were made more comfortable and the plain benches in the pit and gallery were given backs; all the statuettes and ornaments were cleaned and burnished and there were new drop curtains. Irving made the Lyceum into an inviting theatre, staging glittering performances. The audience responded: on first nights the Strand was jammed with carriages.

Irving further enhanced the Lyceum by turning one of its vast rooms into the Beefsteak Room and entertaining well-known figures there. To celebrate the hundredth performance of *The Merchant of Venice* on 14th February 1880, for instance, he asked 300 guests to a five-course banquet, giving them souvenir copies of the play bound in white vellum and lettered in gold. It was the first of the enormous gatherings held at the theatre after the first nights and which became an institution. There was considerable angling for invitations. Despite the lavish invitations to the Lyceum, however, Irving was a reserved man and had only a small circle of friends. Ellen said that he never discussed his intimate thoughts with them.

By transforming the Lyceum in this way, Irving attracted an intellectual middle and upper class audience who came to expect a high standing of acting and drama. In the early and mid 19th century, the working class had formed the majority of theatre audiences. Now this class began to turn to the music halls and to playhouses which staged a mixture of farce and burlesque and still used a declamatory style of acting.

The Merchant of Venice ran for seven months, which was an unprecedented record in the history of the stage. Towards the end of May, Irving decided to cut the last, fifth, act and substitute a new version of *King Rene's Daughter*, by W G Wills, called *Iolanthe*. This was done entirely to give Ellen a chance to play the heroine, a blind girl whose sight is miraculously restored and contrast her

101

strong role as Portia with her 'pathetic' part as Iolanthe. Ellen's performance proved highly popular with audiences but far from pleased everyone. F J Furnivall, the founder of the Shakespearean Society, wrote in a fury to Irving to protest against his 'damnable barbarianism.'

At the end of the second season on 31ˢᵗ July 1880, the receipts again proved excellent. Ellen went off on her third provincial tour with her husband. She remembered a scene they did together in a play called *Butterfly*, which involved a man (acted by Kelly) showing a locket to a dying woman, with a picture of her child in it. They had been using a property locket, but Kelly bought a silver one and inserted real photos of Edy and Teddy and Ellen promptly burst into real tears.

Despite this intimacy, the relationship between the two of them had been deteriorating for some time. They played Beatrice and Benedict respectively in *Much Ado About Nothing*, but their strife on stage was echoed by equal strife off stage.

Ellen was noticeably reticent as to the reason for this in her memoirs, but her daughter commented later that her second husband had no intention of playing second fiddle as an actor. 'He fancied himself as a leading man.' This implies the presumption that he was mortified by her engagement at the Lyceum, which threatened his position as her leading man. It is known that he resented the friendship with Henry Irving which was the sequel to the engagement.'[23] His drinking, always a liability, increased. Shortly after the tour ended, in the late autumn of 1880, he asked Ellen for a divorce.

A divorce in those days was lengthy and publicly embarrassing and Ellen was in no position to invite further scandal. Fortunately Kelly agreed to a legal separation the following year. Ellen was profoundly thankful their marriage was now at an end. Years later Bernard Shaw suggested that Ellen might like to play Julia, the jealous heroine of his play *The Philanderer* and Ellen told him she could play the character to the life, if she played it: 'For three years I lived with a male Julia. He was my husband, Mr Wardell ("Charles Kelly") and I'm alive! But I should have died had I lived one more month with him. I gave him three-quarters of all the money I made weekly, and prayed him to go.'[24] It sounds generous enough, but until the passing of the Married Women's Property Act in 1881, Ellen's money was technically under Kelly's control. Her son queried why they had ever married: 'Certainly not love—admiration?' He presumed she was trying to find a father for himself and his sister 'AND a sort of hefty protector for herself—and a practical daily assistant.'[25] But he admitted to being puzzled as to why the two of them had separated.

There seems no reason why he should be so sure that it was 'Certainly not love'. Ellen, on the rebound from Godwin, may well have thought that she was in love with Kelly, who was undoubtedly an attractive man. But her son would have been too young at the time of their marriage to have understood the problems that his mother faced with her second husband.

Kelly's drinking and jealously only grew with Ellen's meteoric rise at the Lyceum and were not initially so apparent. However, Ellen was constantly rehearsing, constantly tired and Kelly was offered no work at the Lyceum by Irving. It was not a recipe for a happy marriage.

Neighbours of Ellen's at Longridge Road were pleased to note the disappearance of Kelly, having long watched with interest as Ellen left for the theatre every morning to rehearse. 'She appeared upon the steps like April morning, lifting wide eloquent lips, hooded eyes and breathless face to the light. She raised and kissed two little tots who were to be known as Edith and Gordon Craig.' They felt that Kelly, the 'manly bulldog sort of man' did not fit in. 'We resented the conjunction for her as a false consort.' After a year the substantial figure of Kelly disappeared and a new figure was welcomed in Longridge Road, 'spare, and grim-jaunty in close-fitting short jacket, and tilted wide-a-wake; Henry Irving.'[26]

Ellen's relationship with Irving must indeed have been hard for her husband to accept. Professionally, it was very strong: they admired each other's work, and gave each other support. Above all, they shared a passionate interest in what they were trying to achieve. Although Irving had the final say, they spent many hours intensely discussing the plays and their respective parts. Their separate dressing rooms were next to each other: they spent much of the day and evening at the Lyceum and for both it became their virtual home.

The clear electricity existing between Ellen and Irving on stage, their mutual, total involvement in their work, the euphoria of their success, Ellen's mystical beauty and Irving's romantic disposition—all this points to them being lovers off stage. Sir Donald Sinden tells me that he saw some letters written by Irving to Ellen which, at the time, were owned by the antiquarian bookseller, Ifan Kyrle Fletcher. They were then bought by an American professor from Princeton University and subsequently they disappeared. Sir Donald says that the content of these letters made it absolutely clear that Irving was having an affair with Ellen.

Ellen wrote of Irving: 'I have never seen in living man, or picture, such distinction of bearing. A splendid figure, and his face very noble. A superb brow; rather small dark eyes which can at moments become immense, and hang like a bowl of dark liquid with light shining through, a most refined curving Roman nose, strong and delicate in line, and cut clean (as all his features); a smallish mouth, and full of the most wonderful teeth…lips most delicate and refined—firm, firm, firm—and with a rare smile of the most exquisite beauty, and quite-not-to-be described kind… never have I seen such hands.'[27]

Being Irving's leading lady both on and off stage brought her a mixture of happiness and unhappiness. In her private life, even at her happiest, she resented Irving's egotism which in the theatre she admired.

The few loving notes that do remain from him, however, show his deep feelings for her almost amounted to infatuation. One undated fragment reads: 'Soon—Soon! I shall be near you on Sunday. God bless you, my only thought. Your own till Death.'[28] Another note from him, which Ellen pasted inside her copy of *Hamlet*, reads: 'My fairest—sweetest, loveliest Ophelia. Only this. Your Hamlet.' After sending her a schedule of forthcoming Lyceum plays, Irving was to say: 'We must bring the summer to ourselves by being together as often as we can'; a further ended 'You gave me a lovely letter to take away with me on Monday—My own dear wife as long as I live'; and another kept by her son closed with, 'Goodbye my dearest life for one, two, three days. Each morning is a bright one now.'[29] After the opening of a play called *The Amber Heart* a note from Irving to Ellen began, 'You were very lovely my darling—You yourself—alone—and there is nothing in the world beside you I wish we could talk it over now—together—I think I could tell you of the dream of beauty that you realised and were. A lovely night of rest and peace is the wish of your own fond love'.[30]

Ellen's daughter commented that if these letters were really sincere, Irving clearly loved her mother, although she added that 'he loved himself and his calling as an actor, which were really inseparable, more.'

Margaret Webster, whose parents were members of the Lyceum company, said that her mother never had the slightest doubt that they were lovers and would have been amazed at anyone believing their association was merely professional.[31] Sir Donald Sinden was similarly told by the actor Alan Aynesworth, who knew Ellen well, that her affair with Irving was well known.

Marguerite Steen said that when Ellen was in her sixties she asked her outright if she had been Irving's mistress. 'Of course I was', Ellen had replied. 'We were terribly in love for a while. Then, later on, when it didn't matter so much to me, he wanted us to go on, and so I did, because I was very, very fond of him and he said he needed me.' She said that stage love scenes, after they were lovers off-stage, embarrassed her. 'I felt stiff and self-conscious and found myself blushing from head to foot—which was very difficult for Henry!'[32] Ellen also wrote from Chicago to her sister Marion to say, 'This is the first time Henry and I are staying in different Hotels and we are both dull for that—but I cd not stay in the middle of the City, and he took his rooms two months ago.'[33]

Irving, as a married man, was in no position to make Ellen his wife. His legal wife refused to divorce him although, in the 1880s, Irving tried to negotiate a legal separation. Aware of the closeness of her husband to Ellen, his wife would have been delighted to catch him out in adultery. She always referred to Ellen as 'the creature' or 'the wench.' Her son emphatically insisted that Ellen and Irving were never lovers, but Edy in private said that they were.

One argument against their being lovers was that Irving could not afford the notoriety of a divorce and, intent on striving to bring respectability to the theatre which was still regarded as an immoral occupation, he must have realised that an open affair with Ellen would have destroyed all his work. Yet given his barren relationship with his own wife, when he was banned from even seeing his two small sons who were brought up to hate him, he must have longed to come home to Ellen's warmth and charm.

Ellen, in turn, was equally well aware of the stigma attached to impropriety. She now had a divorce and a separation behind her, seven years of illicit living with Edward Godwin and two children born illegitimately. A further open and irregular relationship could have been disastrous. Fortunately for her, there were no tabloids splashing gossip around and following her with a telephoto lens.

Although she cared little for conventions, after her years of social rejection she was aware of just how carefully she had to tread in those conforming times. She would never have dreamed of visiting Irving alone in his rooms at Grafton Street. Nevertheless, she had already broken the Victorian code of behaviour and society regarded her as a fallen woman, even if more sinned against than sinning.

Those who doubt the closeness of Ellen's relationship and believe that Irving was never her lover point to her lifelong love for Godwin. Indeed a crucifix made by her son, and at her bedside when she died, had written on the bottom 'EWG—1886 the 6 Oct. My love (and my only lover) died. God rest his soul.'

Laurence Irving, in his biography of his grandfather Henry, believed that the strait-laced and censorious mid-Victorian London society, which welcomed Ellen and Irving into their circle, was certainly unaware of any liaison. Both he and Ellen's niece Olive were convinced that the two were loving friends but did not actually consummate their relationship.

However, Ted, Ellen's son, remembers that on Sundays his mother invariably drove off to her cottage at Hampton Court with Irving, 'waving her lily white hand.' Once, when Irving was staying at another of Ellen's cottages in Winchelsea, she warmed his cold feet on her stomach under her dress. Ellen trod a fine line here.

Laurence Irving believed that Henry Irving looked on Ellen as a gifted, but irresponsible daughter 'adored, spoiled, and often rebuked with unexpected severity.' Ellen's love for Irving, he thought, was more of a mother who took pride in her son's genius,

Teddy had been named Edward Gordon. Like his sister he later adopted the surname Craig, an idea of Ellen's after she saw the Scottish rock, Ailsa Craig.

but who had to counter his faults. He admits, though, that to Irving, Ellen was always the 'Queen of every woman' and that he adored her 'with an adoration deeper than that of a self-centred artist for an indispensable and much admired colleague.'[34]

Jealous of his dignity, Irving was likely to have scorned the necessary subterfuge an affair required. Laurence Irving says there was a time when Irving, recklessly considering divorce in the

Ellen and Edy. Doting mother though she was, Ellen soon realised that Edy was an uncompromising child. Their later relationship was to sour at times.

hope that Ellen would marry him, bought The Grange, a house in Brook Green, west London. He designed the garden on the lines of the garden Ellen had in Harpenden, possibly considering it a possible home for the two of them. It was never lived in.

Ellen was remarkably level-headed and would have looked carefully at the pros and cons of marrying Irving. She confessed she never came to know the real Irving and was aware that her importance to him was a curious mixture of professional and personal. Her son remembers her commenting, 'Yes, yes—were I to be run over by a steamroller tomorrow, Henry would be deeply grieved: would say quietly, "What a pity!" and would add, after two moments' reflection: "Who is there—er—to go on for her tonight?" Crucially, as Laurence Irving points out, 'The dominant factor in their relationship was their wholehearted admiration of each other as artists.'[35]

Henry endeared himself to Ellen by his kindness to her children. Her son said that he 'proved as kind as a father' and called down 'a thousand blessings on the coming of H I' as he was beginning to feel something was wrong, 'brought about by the so many dear women all around me...never a word from them of my father. Every other boy I knew had his mother and father.'[36]

Ellen was not due to return to the Lyceum until the end of the year, so Irving opened the autumn 1880 season on 18th September with a curtain raiser one-act new play by Pinero, followed by an old favourite, *The Corsican Brothers*, in which he played both parts. Henry James apostrophised the play as hackneyed and preposterous. Irving meanwhile had asked Tennyson to write a new play for the Lyceum and Tennyson obliged by writing *The Cup*, an adaptation of a story by Plutarch in which Camma, whose husband has been jealously assassinated by a Galatian tyrant, offers the tyrant a cup of poisoned wine to avoid seduction.

Ellen and her daughter Edy both attended the reading of the play that winter by Tennyson, Edy then aged nine, sitting on Irving's knee, along with Hallam, Tennyson's son, and William Terriss, the actor who would play Camma's husband. Tennyson read in a monotone, rumbling way, then suddenly switched to a high key for the women's parts. To Ellen's embarrassment, Edy started laughing and Irving then joined in.

Ellen later wrote to her sister Kate from her Hampton Court cottage to say she was down there without a soul to speak to see what she could do with Camma. She said she had begun to like the play even better but 'I hear Daddy doesn't think much of it. We'll see.'

The Cup opened on 3rd January 1881. Ellen considered the production, with its lighting effects, was one of the most beautiful she had ever seen. Much of the credit for this was due to Godwin's archaeological research and his artistic adaptation. Tennyson praised Ellen's 'noble, most beautiful and imaginative rendering of Camma' and Labouchere, writing in *Truth*, light-heartedly praised Irving for engaging Ellen, the idol of the artists, as she embodied the aspirations of modern art as 'with her waving movements and skill at giving life to drapery, she is the actress of all others to harmonise with gold backgrounds and to lounge under blossoming apple trees.'[37]

Godwin wrote an affectionate note to her during a performance of the play, with illustrations of the archaeological attitudes that are justifiably correct for an actress to use: 'This, and this, but never that.'

The drama played to packed audiences for 125 nights. It preceded *The Corsican Brothers*, which made the evening rather weighty but to Ellen's relief as she was tiring of tragedy, Irving substituted the comedy *The Belle's Stratagem* for *The Corsican Brothers*. It gave Ellen a chance to play comedy and tragedy each night.

Ellen returned to tragedy on 3rd May, when Irving launched *Othello*. She enjoyed playing Desdemona, however, saying 'there was something of the nun in her.' Irving and Edwin Booth alternated weekly as Othello and Iago. Irving was praised for his Iago and condemned for his Othello: even Ellen agreed that he screamed and ranted and raved in the part. Irving was conscious of his own failure, rolling up the clothes he wore as the Moor on the last night and saying, with a relieved sigh, 'Never again.'

Ellen, visiting her father after playing Desdemona, was shocked when he said to her, 'We must have no more of these Ophelias and Desdemona's', and asked him what he meant by it. Her father replied, 'They're second fiddle parts—not the parts for you, Duchess.' Ellen, who had enjoyed playing Ophelia in particular and had

110

been delighted at her success in it, argued that this had been a 'first fiddle' part, along with her part in *Olivia* and *The Cup*.

Ellen's friends and admirers fiercely agreed with her father, pointing, for instance, to the way Ellen never had a chance to play Rosalind as Irving did not consider there was a suitable part for himself in *As You Like It*. But her friends were ambitious for her: Ellen herself had never been ambitious and indeed, no one who was could have remained working under such an autocratic manager as Irving. Ellen knew her own worth and was confident that Irving was anxious for her success. However she was also aware that in making his decisions, he did not take her into account so much as the overall success of the Lyceum company. She admitted to Clement Scott, the critic that 'My aim is usefulness to my lovely art and to Henry Irving. This is not a very high ambition, is it? But long ago I gave up dreaming, and I think I see things as they are—especially see myself as I am, alas!, both off and on the stage, and I only aspire to help a little.'[39]

Bernard Shaw, in later years, angrily condemned Ellen for allowing Irving to dominate her, though had few parts to offer her when she finally left the Lyceum. He failed to understand that Ellen was perfectly happy deferring to Irving. She was always prepared to defer to men she admired, like Watts and Godwin. She sat for hours modelling for Watts and spent an equal amount of time tracing Godwin's architectural drawings. Never did she regard that time as being wasted, as a time when instead of helping others, she could have been practising her own art. She often said that she was more woman than artist, then would contradict herself by saying how much she loved to work. It was a conflict she never solved.

On rare occasions Ellen did argue with Irving, although he was as unyielding to her as to everyone else. Once, about a year after she joined the Lyceum, the two had a lengthy, intense altercation over the precise line in a play at which the curtain should descend. Ellen summoned up every artistic argument she could, imploring him to change his mind, but he remained obdurate. After holding out for a week, she gave in. 'It's my duty to obey your orders and do it', she said, 'but I do it under protest.'

Ellen did not consider she would have achieved more success

Ellen's portrayal of Juliet in the 1882 production of Romeo and Juliet *drew criticism that she lacked the tragic passion required for the part.*

without Henry Irving. 'I might have had "bigger" parts, but it doesn't follow that they would have been better ones, and if they had been written by contemporary dramatists my success would have been less durable.'[40] Graham Robertson emphatically shared her view. In a letter he wrote in 1931, he said: 'As to her [Ellen's] career being sacrificed to him (Irving)—does anyone in their senses suppose that she would have gained her unique position without him? She has little ambition—no 'push'—little business capacity. She loved to serve and would always have served somebody.'[41]

Margaret Webster, whose parents acted with Ellen, considered that 'Irving's genius as a director, his ordering of the whole, the steel in him, perfectly complemented her own radiance and the outgoing zest for life which streamed from her.'[42]

In 1882, when Irving decided to stage *Romeo and Juliet*, he was 44 years old and Ellen was 35. She worried that she was neither young enough nor old enough to play Juliet. She thought it the greatest opportunity she had yet had at the Lyceum but after studying the part in the bedroom of her cottage at Hampton Court she said, 'I wish now that instead of reading how this and that actress had played Juliet, and cracking my brain over the different readings of her lines and making myself familiar with the different opinions of philosophers and critics, I had gone to Verona, and just imagined'.[43]

She was accused of persuading Irving to do the play as it would be virtually her last chance, but as Irving's grandson said, no one ever managed to over-persuade Irving. It was more likely he wanted to fulfil his ambition for Ellen. He seriously considered playing Mercutio instead, but could find no other actor he considered could play Romeo.

The first night on 8th March 1882 was attended by the Prince and Princess of Wales. Irving's wife, Florence, in her usual box wrote cattily in her diary that night, 'First night of *Romeo and Juliet* at Lyceum—jolly failure—Irving awfully funny.' *The Athenaeum* considered that although Ellen played with her usual grace, beauty and intelligence, her Juliet was 'altogether inferior to her Ophelia, and far below her Portia.' *The Saturday Review* commented that Ellen 'is very charming, but she is not Juliet; and when really tragic passion is wanted for the part, it is not forthcoming.' Sarah Bernhardt praised her performance, however, especially her 'real tears', and Irving was equally complimentary. He told Ellen he had seen her mother at the first night, looking radiant. 'I told her how proud she should be, and she was.' After the dress rehearsal, he had written to her saying, 'Beautiful as Portia was, Juliet leaves her far,

far behind. Never anybody acted more exquisitely the part.'[45]

Ellen in turn sprang to Irving's defence when one critic told her that he was an unrealistic Romeo, retorting that 'the worst thing Henry Irving could do, would be better than the best of anyone else.' The play drew good houses despite poor notices and ran for 160 performances.

In retrospect she thought her interpretation failed because of her lack of original impulse. She also felt that she did not *look* right as Juliet. Her daughter told her that she oughtn't to have a fringe.

Ellen retrieved her reputation after her Juliet when, on 11th October that year, she played Beatrice in *Much Ado about Nothing*. After studying Beatrice, Ellen was convinced she was ruled by both mind and heart. She was struck by her pride 'pride without an ounce of vanity. Vanity makes women feeble—pride makes them strong.' She also admired Beatrice's chivalry in thinking of her cousin's wrongs despite Benedict having just told her of his love.

The critics could not think of sufficiently ecstatic adjectives to describe Ellen's performance, often considered her best. Her son Teddy, now nine, excitedly watched her from the stage box on the first night. He held Irving in reverence, regarding him in the light of a father. It was natural enough: not only was Irving very kind to both children but Godwin's name had been long kept from Teddy by Ellen and the other women looking after him. 'Never a word from them of my father', he said. 'Not having mine—not hearing of mine—this grave sensation of something being wrong grew and grew into a fixed sort of small terror with me.'[46]

In the January of 1883, Teddy started boarding school at Southfields Park near Tunbridge Wells in Kent. Run by the Reverend Ernest Wilkinson, Southfields Park was a solid house set in fields. Teddy's first letter home, on 29th January, read:

'Darling Mother, We were met by Mr Wilkinson at the station. Only two out of 12 are gentleman that is the boy that came down with me and Myself. I don't like the School very much the lessons are very nice. The boy's wanted to see my desk and they wanted to see something I did not want them to see so they took my thing witch holds my pen and pencle and paper knife I don't think I shall get it back. Good by Mother Your loving boy, Teddy.'[47]

Another letter in the same week started, 'I feel so unhappy,

114

Mother...' Ellen wrote on it, '1883—1st week at school—Poor Kid. E T'. However, life soon improved. He wrote on 10th February to say: 'We have fine larks now' and again on 18th March to say, 'I like the school very much. It is "Rare Jolly"—that is our Word.' Ellen replied saying she was sending him 'one jolly good Hamper' which was going to include two cakes, two boxes of sardines, some biscuits, bon-bons, jam, toffy and oranges.

Edy meanwhile had become a boarder at Mrs Cole's school which by now had grown in size and reputation and moved into larger premises. Later she went to Gloucestershire to continue her education at the home of Mrs Cole's sister, Mrs Malleson.

Much Ado About Nothing played to crowded houses but was withdrawn in June 1883. Irving had decided to take the entire company over to America on tour and the organising of a hundred-strong company, plus scenery, took time.

In late August, before leaving on the tour, Ellen and Irving carried out a six-week provincial tour. In Scotland the two of them along with Irving's secretary Bram Stoker and Ted went on a boat trip around the famous rock, Ailsa Craig. 'What a good stage name!' said Ellen. 'A pity you can't have it, Ted. I shall give it to Edy.'[48] Edy did indeed use the name Ailsa Craig on her first stage appearance, then found another actress with that name. She changed Ailsa back to Edith, though kept the surname Craig. Ted, christened at 16, was given the names Edward (after his father), Henry (after his godfather Irving) and Gordon (after his godmother Lady Gordon). He registered his name as Edward Henry Gordon Craig by deed poll when he was 21 and was known as Gordon Craig for the rest of his life.

At the time, though, in the autumn of 1883 while his mother tearfully set sail for America, he and Edy climbed out of the bedroom window of the friends' house where they were staying and sat on the old red roof eating biscuits and fruit and chocolates. Edy was then 13, he was 11. 'I was never happier than when with Edy', he said.

115

Conquering America

Irving decided to take the Lyceum Company to tour America in 1882 as a way of raising money for London performances. Ellen was alternatively thrilled and despairing at the idea of the visit, but she was immensely successful and was to return to America on tour a number of times.

Ellen had a passion for dogs, especially fox terriers. The two terriers pictured, Drummie (left) and Fussie, accompanied her everywhere. She gave Fussie to Henry Irving and the two became inseparable companions.

Conquering America

The Lyceum company left for their first tour of America in the autumn of 1883. It was the first of Ellen's eight tours there, seven of which were with Henry Irving. The last tour she made was in 1907, after his death. Ellen calculated she had spent nearly five years of her life in America.

The first tour, however, caused immense excitement though some of the English papers derided Irving's ambition. When he had taken on the American actor, Edwin Booth, to play at the Lyceum, his patronage was attacked as being self-serving. One cartoon showed Booth and Irving arm in arm, with Booth pondering, 'What does all this tarnation civility mean, I wonder?' and Irving in an aside saying, 'This move will be certain to pull me through when I visit America.'[1]

Despite this snide reaction to the forthcoming tour, Irving was now eminent enough to be given a farewell banquet attended by distinguished guests at the old St James's Hall in Piccadilly. Despite the male-only tradition of banquets, Ellen was graciously permitted to attend. Graham Robertson, one of the guests, commented that 'A fairer vision than Ellen Terry, then at the zenith of her loveliness, cannot be imagined. She shone with no shallow sparkle or glitter, but with a steady radiance that filled the room, and had the peculiar quality of making everyone else invisible.'[2]

Irving was determined that this first tour by the Lyceum Company would remain in American memory. He arranged to ship over all the scenery and properties of his productions, along with the entire company and staff from the Lyceum. The expenses were enormous but in the end proved a worthwhile gamble as the company made a clear profit of £50,000—an enormous sum for those days. It enabled him to fund the following season at the Lyceum and he was to depend on future American tours to do likewise.

Such a princely method of touring also gave Irving and Ellen a stature they may not have attained merely by their acting. When travelling by train, Irving himself had a private parlour while the Lyceum company and the baggage occupied eight cars, including two 60-foot box cars, a huge gondola to carry the scenery and 150 stage baskets. It proved too costly and some of the scenery was sent back to New York, with scene-painters and carpenters hired instead in individual cities.

Ellen was alternatively thrilled and despairing at the idea of the visit. For six weeks before leaving, she would burst into tears if anyone mentioned America: 'I was leaving my children, my bullfinch, my parrot... to face the unknown dangers of the Atlantic and of a strange, barbarous land.'[3] Audiences at the Lyceum shared her emotions, cheering, crying and throwing bouquets and laurel leaves at the farewell performance. On setting sail from Liverpool to New York on 11th October 1882, Ellen tearfully waved goodbye to well-wishers who included Oscar Wilde and Lily Langtry.

Despite the ship being laden with pig-iron and rolling incessantly, Ellen described the journey as 'a voyage of enchantment' and was equally delighted with her first view of New York's harbour. She had expected New York to be an 'ugly, noisy place', where the 'American women wore red flannel shirts and carried bowie knives', and where 'I might be sandbagged in the street!' The American papers all praised their first glimpse of her on arrival even though, after Irving had urged her to 'Say something pleasant! Merry and bright!', Ellen in a sudden onset of loneliness, burst into tears. 'A woman of extreme nervous sensibility' was the press verdict.

Finding her hotel room full of roses cheered her and her next tears in America were when she was leaving. There was, in any case, no time for repining as the company had a bare week after their arrival in which to set up and rehearse the plays they were to

Ellen in New York. An unseasoned traveller, on her first visit there she had expected American women to wear red flannel shirts and carry bowie knives.

present, including *The Bells, Charles I, Hamlet, The Belle's Stratagem, Richard III, The Lyons Mail, Louis XI, The Merchant of Venice* and *Much Ado About Nothing.*

The company opened at the Star Theatre on 29th October 1883 with Irving's legendary *The Bells*. The audience, Ellen found, was 'a splendid one—discriminating and appreciative. We felt that the Americans *wanted* to like us.' She noted that in America in 1883 the productions of romantic plays and Shakespeare that Irving brought over were unknown. 'We were the first and we were pioneers, and we were new. To be new is everything in America.' It accounted for the extraordinary success of the first tour.

Ellen's first appearance on the following night was as Henrietta Maria in *Charles I*. Although she considered she had played badly, and cried too much in the last act, the audience 'were instantly enslaved by her charm' and vociferously applauded both her and the play. She was impressed that throughout their tour, the critics were keenly interested in the plays Irving had chosen and showed a scholarly knowledge of many points passed over by English critics. She was similarly impressed by the culture of American women, 'by the evidence that they had read far more and developed a more fastidious taste than most young English women.'

Washington was the first city she had come across where the men didn't just stay in the background 'untiringly turning out the dollars', but actually contributed to the social life. She was equally aware of 'the vivacity, the appearance, at least, of reality, the animation, the energy of American women.'[4]

The third play staged was *Louis XI* and Irving's power of characterisation in his portrayal of the old French king was greeted with wonder. The last week at the Star Theatre was full to capacity. Critics were divided into three factions: those who thought Irving a genius; those who were aware of his eccentricities but were still carried away by enthusiasm; and those who found him and his company unacceptable. Irving was particularly pleased at the tributes received from American actors. But the public were equally delighted. Irving's *Hamlet* in Philadelphia received a phenomenally enthusiastic reception.

On this first tour, the company visited New York, Philadelphia, Boston, Baltimore, Chicago, Cincinnati, Columbus, St Louis, Detroit, Washington, the larger towns of New England and Toronto. The pace was furious and they even had to work on Christmas Day, when they opened in Baltimore in thick snow. Ellen put up holly and mistletoe in the hotel and produced a Christmas pudding made by her mother.

The tour ended in New York with a three-week run of *Much Ado about Nothing* to applauding audiences. In his farewell speech, Irving thanked his audience and all America for showing 'that no jealous

Ellen's portrayal of Viola in 1884 was considered enchanting, though she considered the production dull and lumpen. A poisoned finger forced her to leave the production.

love of your own most admirable actors had prevented you from recognising the earnest purpose of an English company.'[5] He was asked to what he attributed his success. 'To my acting,' he replied.

Irving, exhilarated by the resounding success the company had achieved, wrote to his secretary Louis Frederick Austin, who had remained in England to look after company matters, to say that their success had been beyond precedent so he had decided the company would return to America for a second tour the following September. He added that Ellen 'was even better than she ever was

123

in dear old England and has had a glorious and brilliant success', winning golden opinions from all and sundry.

Ellen and Irving and the Lyceum company sailed back to England in the April of 1883, landing on 8th May. The following day, *The Times* formally welcomed him back. Ellen said that on her return to London she was hurt by 'the hopeless look on so many faces; the dejection and apathy of the people standing about in the streets.'

Her children had missed her. Teddy, apparently set on following in his mother's theatrical footsteps, wrote to her on 17th May to say, 'Darling Mother, We are going to act Bluebeard here and I am going to act Bluebeard. Please ask Arnott (the Lyceum carpenter) to make me a wooden sword nicely finished and curved a good shape.'6

The sixth season at the Lyceum was going to be a comparatively short one as the company was returning to America in just four months. Irving wanted to open at the Lyceum with a play by a new English dramatist and indeed spent £3,000 looking for new material. There was, however, a dearth of new playwrights and the deaths of two popular ones, Charles Reade and H J Byron, which took place during the American tour, had worsened matters. In the end the sixth season opened with a brief revival of *Much Ado About Nothing*, in which Ellen was rapturously welcomed, followed by *Twelfth Night*, which opened on 8th July 1884.

Most unusually, Irving was barracked, booed and hissed when giving his speech on stage at the end of the play.

He reacted furiously, saying he failed to understand criticism of actors who were 'sober, clean and perfect.' He eventually calmed the audience with the remark 'In your smiles we are happy, prithee smile upon us.' His Malvolio provoked contrary opinions though Ellen's Viola was considered by the critic Clement Scott to be 'tender, human, graceful, consistently picturesque, and with humour as light as featherdown.'7

Ellen thought that the first night was not a comedy audience and that 'the rolickings of Toby Belch and his fellows were thought "low." In her opinion, the production was 'dull, lumpy and heavy. Henry's Malvolio was fine and dignified, but not good for the play.' One unusual occurrence was that Ellen did not play both twins,

Ellen at her house in Longridge Road, southwest London, in 1884. Neighbours were fascinated to catch even the flicker of her elbow in the bay window of her dining room. Young, would-be actresses flocked to see her daily.

Viola and Sebastian, herself. Instead her brother Fred, who did indeed look and act like her, played Sebastian with great success.

Unfortunately on the first night Ellen was in agony with such a bad whitlow that she had to wear a sling. Her thumb grew worse each night and she became so sick and faint with the pain that she often had to play her part sitting down. One night the brother of Bram Stoker, Irving's manager, who was a doctor, happened to be backstage, saw it and lanced it immediately. But blood poisoning had set in to such an extent that Ellen nearly lost her arm. Marion Terry took over Ellen's part on stage and Irving ordered straw to be laid down in Longridge Road outside Ellen's house to deaden the sound of passing horses and carriages.

One response was a vicious speech made at the Social Science Congress about 'actresses who feign illness and have straw laid down before their houses, while behind the drawn blinds they are having riotous supper-parties, dancing the can-can and drinking champagne.'[8] Irving obviously still had some way to go before he succeeded in making the stage respectable. He never forgave the speech-maker and if he ever found himself in the same room would walk out.

The play ran its allotted course but to failing interest. At its end, Ellen decided that summer to rent a cottage at Winchelsea in Sussex for herself and her children. Next door was the weekend cottage of Alice Comyns Carr, a friend who was married to the dramatic critic of the *Pall Mall Gazette* and who was soon taken on to design Ellen's stage dresses.

Alice Comyns Carr remembered one of Ellen's favourite pastimes was going out in the early morning, clad only in the flimsiest of long white night-dresses and dancing on the lawn in front of the house. Alice's husband Joe remonstrated with Ellen, pointing out that her unconventional behaviour might shock the neighbours. Ellen merely laughed and replied, 'Who's to see me, Joe, at five o'clock in the morning? There are only the labourers going to work, and I don't mind amusing them. It's so good for the poor dears.'

She surprised him by enthusiastically joining in the village theatricals. Asked at first rather timidly if she would give her patronage to these she replied, 'Patronage? Nonsense! Why, I'll do the whole thing if you like.' Alice Comyns Carr said she never forgot 'the feeling of incongruity which overcame me as I watched Ellen Terry, fresh from her Shakespearean triumphs, going through ancient amateur gags in the bare and comfortless stone hall at Winchelsea, with the rows of smelly oil lamps for footlights.'[9]

Henry Irving often came down as Ellen's guest and Blanche Patch, the Rector of Winchelsea's daughter and later Bernard Shaw's secretary for 30 years, commented that in those days without motorcars and when a trip to London was an event, very few knew of his fame as an actor. His presence in Ellen's house, however, 'did not lessen the doubts of those ladies who held fast

126

Irving with his beloved Fussie, a gift from Ellen, at Ellen's Winchelsea cottage. Fussie died in true theatrical style by falling through a stage trapdoor.

to Victorian taboos about whether a London actress was the sort of person who should be "called on".'[10]

The summer break did not last long. On 18th September 1884 the Lyceum company set sail once more for America. The profits of such a tour had become necessary as, for the first time, the last Lyceum season in London had worryingly shown a slight loss.

The company encountered violent storms at sea and Ellen was more dead than alive when the company opened at Quebec on 30th September. L F Austin, Irving's secretary, wrote home to his wife to say that once the miseries of the voyage were over, everyone was in top spirits and 'Ellen seemed to lose the terrible weariness which had nearly quenched the light in her eyes.' He described the Quebec theatre as being 'a cross between a chapel and a very small concert room' and that they had been taken aback when 'we found two members of the preceding troupe on stage—they were two hens.'[11]

The play they opened with was *Parisian* and was wildly applauded. The company moved on to Montreal where the theatre was again crammed with a delighted audience. But Ellen collapsed and had to stay behind, only catching up with the company in Toronto.

Once back in the United States, the actors repeated their success. In New York, where Irving played *Hamlet*, receipts were higher than before. The Christmas of 1884 was spent in Pittsburg. The Christmas plum pudding Ellen had brought with her was a complete failure as it reeked of camphor, having been accidentally packed along with her furs. But she was delighted to find that the male members of the company had clubbed together to buy her a silver tea service. 'E T's face I shall never forget', wrote L F Austin to his wife. 'The surprise, the pleasure, and the choking emotion made her such a picture as she never has looked on the stage. Then she stood up, with great tears rolling down her cheeks—while Henry tried to conceal his behind his glasses—and said a few broken words more eloquent than any speech.'[12]

Ellen cabled to her friend Stephen Coleridge who was leaving for New York to 'bring over one of the children.' He chose Teddy. It was a curious thing to do, leaving the decision to Coleridge. Possibly she felt that she could not that way be accused of favouritism.

Austin, who went to meet him, told his wife he never saw a nicer lad. 'He is a perfect little gentleman.' Teddy was given a sledge and every time the train stopped Austin took it out in the snow and gave him a ride. Henry refused to join in, staying on the steps of the train car 'with a tragic air' unlike Ellen who 'was just like a schoolgirl, every bit as young in feeling as her boy.'

Ellen was to say that when she played Ophelia in Chicago for the first time, she played the part better than she ever had before. She was further delighted by a comment from a Chicago drama critic that Teddy, who had a walk-on part in *Eugene Aram,* had eyes 'full of sparkle, his smile is a ripple over his face, and his laugh is as cheery and natural as a bird's song.'

Teddy might be with her, but Ellen missed Edy and, obviously aware she must feel left out, constantly wrote to her. One letter to her daughter on 17th March assured her that all Ellen's American friends 'are ready to love you for yourself alone. She then gave her maternal advice on her drawing:

'I don't like your dog's head as well as a little sketch you once did of Fussie and Charlie, but the flower was very pretty…meanwhile observe all angles in natural objects and proportion, note too the unequal balance in flower-life and shell—all will be of use to you should you one day for instance play Lady Macbeth! I'll explain 'because why' when we meet, my little noodlemus—Please study Jessica *(M of V)* next (what a comedown) and get done with the only, to my mind, Cat in Shakspere. It is a very effective part tho' played properly and "looked" as you could look it. Poor Ted has a little cruel pain in his little stom-ack and I must go and make a fuss of him and rub it!! Your own Mummy.'[13]

In Boston, Irving became ill and box office receipts fell dramatically from $1,900 to $500, but by the time the company sailed home on 9th April 1885, they had made a clear profit of £15,000.

On Ellen's return she found that her second husband, Charles Wardell, had died on 17th April. Generous as ever, she paid all his debts and continued to support the sisters of his first wife for years. At the time, however, she immediately had to plunge into rehearsal for the opening of the seventh Lyceum season in May and hardly had time to mourn him.

A revival of *Hamlet* was followed by a further revival of *Olivia*. Ellen's comments on this production show her assessment of plays was sharp and knowledgeable. She was critical of Irving altering the last act. 'The division into two scenes wasted time, and nothing was gained by it.' She was relieved that Irving realised this and restored the orginal. 'It was weak and unsatisfactory but not pretentious and bad like the last act he presented at the first performance.'[14] She also considered Irving played his part too slowly, thereby slowing down the whole tempo of the play.

His early rehearsals were poor and on one occasion Edy, watching him stamp his foot as if he were playing his melodramatic part in *The Bells,* said frankly, 'Don't go on like that, Henry. Why don't you talk as you do to me and Teddy? At home you are the vicar.' Irving was not annoyed, finding her criticism illuminating, and immediately played the part more simply.

In the May of 1886 Ted went off to Bradfield College, a public school where he claimed to have learnt very little Latin and no

Greek or Maths. That July, Edward Godwin advised on the production of *The Fool's Revenge* at the Opera Comique. It was his last work: the following month he went into St Peter's Hospital and on 6th October he died.

As architect, he had completed some memorable civic buildings, but one of his best known successes was the 'White House' in Chelsea for his friend, the artist James Whistler. Oscar Wilde called him 'one of the most artistic spirits of this century in England.' He had assisted with the designs for London's new Law Courts and the Houses of Parliament in Berlin, but from 1875 when he gave advice on the Bancrofts' production of *The Merchant of Venice*, he became engrossed by his work for the theatre, designing innovative stage sets, costumes and furniture. Yet he nevertheless failed to fulfil his potential.

Edward Craig, Ellen's grandson and son of Gordon Craig and Elena Meo, gave a talk on Godwin called 'E W Godwin, a Magnificent Amateur.' He emphasised that Godwin was fascinatated by seeing the past recreated on stage, but that his abilities did not lie in producing plays. Craig thought there was a cruel streak in Godwin which he considered could have been the lack of recognition he received for his many talents, which included designing public and private buildings, writing art criticism, lecturing on ancient as well as modern costume and making wallpaper, fabric and theatrical designs.

Whistler was with Godwin when he died and according to Ellen's son, asked Mrs Jopling the artist to go to Ellen straightaway and tell her what had happened, to spare her finding it out from the newspapers. It had been some 12 years since she and Godwin had parted, but 'When I told her', said Mrs Jopling, 'I shall never forget her cry: "There was no one like him".'[15]

Ellen wrote out her feelings to her friends. One letter, to Mrs Elsa Palmer on 11th October, begs her not to send round to her at the playhouse, if she went, as she would break down at the sight of a very kind face. She had sent for her children 'or I could not have endured I think. Edward Godwin went away and shut the door behind him. He is gone—and I'm wondering I don't die—One does not get much love and he loved me most. I came away into the country directly I heard from Louise Jopling.' She admitted

130

that having to go up to the theatre each night was good for her but asked Elsa Palmer not to write or speak to her. 'Only just love away at me not because I deserve but for Love's sake.'[16]

Writing to another old friend, said, 'I can never think of him but at his best, and when he died, he thought only so of me. I could never suffer again I think as I have suffered, but I joy in the remembrance of him. He loved me, and I loved him, and that, I suppose, is the reason we so cruelly hurt each other.'[17] A further letter to her friend Bertha Bramly, heavily underlined, read:

'I couldn't write in answer to your last letter—Edward Godwin died just then and I have been finished by that. I shall seem well soon, I think, but I didn't know how terribly it would alter me. I went on at my work for a time but broke down at last and sent for Edith to be with me. Selfish and wrong but I couldn't help it—I think I shd have lost my wits from misery—I'm all right now. Edith did that She and Ted are with me now...Ted my boy has altered lately—looks rather shy now sometimes and is much quieter. Edith the same rum queer old Frump!'[18]

Godwin's wife Beatrice and his two closest friends, Whistler and Lady Archibald Campbell, went with his coffin by train to Oxfordshire and the three of them, with the coffin, transferred to an open farm wagon. As they jolted along the country lanes, they covered the coffin with a cloth and used it as a table for a makeshift meal. The burial was in the corner of an open field at Norleigh, near Witney. No stone marks the spot as his friends knew he strongly objected to gravestones. Ellen was prohibited, according to the code of manners of the time, from paying any public tribute to him. Not long after his death, his widow married Whistler.

Ellen left London for a week and wrote to a friend to say 'I've gone thro' much distress of mind and body that lasted two months, the stress has been too great to bear.' She said she was fighting not to enjoy life 'but just to hold my own.'

That summer she rented Alice Comyns Carr's cottage and eventually bought it. The Comyns Carr's children called her 'Nellen Terry' and she was highly popular with all the other local children, once paying for every child who needed them to have new boots or shoes. Children filled the ponycart she always drove as she hated trains. With them were Ellen's two adored fox terriers,

131

Ellen as Marguerite in Faust *in 1885. She produced a tragic ring which surprised those who thought her act began and ended with grace.*

Charlie and Fussy. Ellen was to give Fussy to Irving as a gift and they became inseparable. She once came upon the two of them sitting in opposite armchairs 'mutually adoring each other.'

Preparations for the production of W G Wills's version of *Faust* that December included, to Ellen's pleasure, a grand tour of Germany. This time the group included both her children as well as the Comyns Carrs and nearly all the properties used in *Faust* were bought in Nuremberg. Alice Comyns Carr studied old German books and prints for ideas for dress designs, but on her return to the Lyceum for rehearsals was taken aback to find herself working for a rather different Irving. 'Gone was the debonair, cheery holiday companion, and in his place was a ruthless autocrat, who brooked no interference from anyone.'[19]

But Irving's note to Ellen from his home in Grafton Street three days before the play began showed none of this:
'No rehearsal this morning for you, my darling.
Last night was a desperate affair from seven till five this morning...
It will be all right–of course–but it is a stern business.
Yes a Good drive today–perhaps you will drive down.
But do not wear yourself out–and you shall not tonight either if I can persuade (you) to take it quietly.
What a worry you are, you see.
With all my love my dearest dearest.'[20]

Faust collected a fair amount of abuse as a 'distorted caricature of Goethe,' and an 'inartistic production'. But Ellen liked her part of Margaret better than any other, Shakespeare aside. She didn't care for Irving's interpretation of Mephistopheles, although he loved the part himself, swirling malevolently out of a billow of smoke clad in crimson. The stage effects outshone any pantomime, indeed almost outshone the actors, with apparitions appearing and disappearing and electrically-wired swords producing sparks which made the audience gasp.

Henry James dismissed its 'pantomimic effects' with scorn but Ellen managed to avoid bathos and was extremely moving in her part. People queued at the stage door to see her arrive and leave. The play proved the greatest of Irving's financial successes: he had daringly spent £8,000 on its production, but it ran for two seasons and after playing Mephistopheles 496 times he had retrieved this amount and made an additional profit of £24,000. Edy acted as one of the angels in *Faust* and Irving's gift to Ellen of flowers on St Valentine's Day included the verse:

White and red roses
Sweet and fresh posies
One bunch for Edy, Angel of mine
One bunch for Nell, my dear Valentine [21]

During the run Lady Duff Gordon met Ellen during a reception on stage. She admitted being immediately captivated by Ellen's

133

charm and called on her at her house in Longridge Road:

'I found her sitting in the midst of a group of girls who were sewing. She was wearing a flowing robe of blue velvet and her fair hair was bound round her head like a coronet…Although I went to the house many times I rarely saw Ellen Terry without her little circle of girls. I think that any one of them would gladly have laid down their lives for her sake. I never knew any woman who possessed in such a degree the art of inspiring affection in her own sex. She was not a young woman then, but she was the friend and confidante of dozens of girls, who adored her and loved to serve her in all sorts of little ways. They would do her shopping for her, arrange the flowers, dress her to go to the theatre, mend her clothes, and write her letters for her.'[22]

She also noticed Irving drifting in and out of the house at all hours and saw how perfectly Ellen understood him and managed him. 'Once or twice I saw him in a towering rage, working himself up to fever heat over something that had happened at the theatre, but she could calm him in a moment.'

On 11th January 1887, Edy was christened at Exeter Cathedral, with Henry Irving acting as godfather. Ellen wrote in her diary 'A private single ceremony by the Bishop for Edith. Strange! Over 30 years ago Father and Mother (with Kate and me) walked (necessity!) from Bristol to Exeter, and now today my child is given half-an-hour's private talk with the Bishop before her confirmation.'[23]

Ellen's performance that summer as the heroine in Alfred Calmour's rather thin 'Poetical Fancy in Three Acts' called *The Amber Heart* again had critics going into hyperbole and Irving told her 'Poor Alfred he thinks its all his own I know and it never will be without you.'[24]

Immediately after the end of the season in the November of 1887, the company left again for New York where it opened with *Faust* as the main attraction. The company then went on to Philadelphia, Chicago and Boston before returning to New York and encountering the historic blizzard of 1887. Expecting the theatre to be shut, Ellen and Irving dined out, then heard the news that an audience was gathering. According to Ellen's son, a dozen male diners took turns at carrying Ellen on their shoulders the 12 blocks to the theatre.

Ellen in 1887. The previous October her erstwhile lover, Edward Godwin, had died at 52, plunging her into depression. 'There was no one like him' she said with a great cry, on hearing the news.

Before leaving England, Ellen had arranged for both Edy and Ted to continue their studies in Germany. Edy went from the Royal Academy of Music in London for further training as a pianist in Berlin. She studied music under Alexis Hollander there and showed decided promise. However, the rheumatism which had plagued her since early childhood prevented a musical career and she returned home to play small parts at the Lyceum.

Teddy went off to Heidelberg College to learn German, writing weekly to his mother to say his tricycle hadn't arrived, the music was as bad there as his last school and he wasn't being taught drawing. He wanted her to arrange for him to have one bath a week instead of fortnightly and if she would ask Edy to send him a list 'of the nice people I am to know and the nasty ones as we have parties in winter and I don't want to know any outsiders.'[25] Unfortunately, he was expelled for some high-jinks behaviour and returned to England, staying with Ben Terry, Ellen's father.

Ellen wrote frequently to Edy, who later wished she had paid more attention to her good advice. In one letter written in 1887, Ellen mentioned the possibility of 18-year-old Edy accompanying her the following year to America:

'And so to America—the going to America is what you most desire? Well then, work away now. You must give up some of your present pleasures, and work at your German, and speak it. I shall not be able to gratify this wish of your heart, which is for your own pleasure, if you don't gratify the wish of my heart (which is for your own benefit) and make good use of the present time, and work.'[26]

Her next letter says, 'My dearest, in the hope that you will work all the harder for this extra "lark", I send you the Sophia dress so that you may go to the Bal Masque. It will arrive in a few days—a wig also.'

She gives yet more advice to her still unsophisticated daughter: 'Remember you must be more reserved with a pack of folk you don't know well (and one changes one's first opinion of some people) than with old friends and people who know you. You know I used long ago to tell you to keep a little steadier in shops and places where strangers were about.' She warned her daughter to drink claret or wine, but on no account to drink beer 'even of the smallest kind' except occasionally 'just to feel German.' Ellen also told Edy she shouldn't have written to a certain German actor, as she would be vexed if anyone thought her vulgar, and asked about the ability of her music and drawing masters.

Despite the overwhelming tiredness she often felt with constant rehearsing, acting and touring, Ellen's thoughts and concerns constantly centred around her children. Writing to her sister Kate on 10th January 1888 from Chicago, she says that Ted's recent letters to her had been lovely. 'Dear lad—his one fault laziness, if he can but conquer that. Edy is really improved.'

She went on to tell Kate, with amusement, that one of the New York papers ('it was a pretty low one') had said, 'Mr Irving tried, but could not, to get Miss Terry into some of the society he was welcomed in' and then 'went on to make some pleasant remarks about (the late) Mr Wardell and Mr Kelly (they always treat him as two people!).' Ellen admitted that the audiences were not as good in Chicago as they expected, even though drawing more people than the Lyceum Theatre in London would hold. She put this down to the 'dime museums', explaining that for a dime 'you may see the fattest woman, the leanest man, the child with the greatest number of noses.'

She added that she was having a very good time as she felt so much better, that everything Russian was 'the thing' in Chicago ('you shd see some ladies at the Five o'clock Teas') and that she was delighted to read what Kate had said of their father and mother. 'Poor old dears—I pray some happy quiet years are for them both yet—there's so much to interest them in common in their many children and grandchildren that it shd hardly be an ordinary going down hill.'[27]

On 26th January she wrote to Teddy to describe her activities: her room was full of bowls and vases and jugs of roses and spring flowers despite the snow outside; that she and Edy were just off on a sleigh drive; that Edy was wonderfully improved in her music and sketching; that she would take four months' rest on her return from the present tour 'previous to coming out (and being cut up!) as Lady Macbeth'; and that she had been terribly hoarse with a cold but Irving had insisted she open in *Faust*.

'I got mad and said "I do think that if your son, or your mother, your wife, the idol of your heart, were to die on the stage through making the effort to do the work, you wd let it happen". "Certainly I would," said he to my amusement. I expected he wd say, "Oh come now, you exaggerate"... He certainly wd drop himself before he'd give in and there my Ted is the simple secret of his great success in everything he undertakes.'[28]

Lady *L* Macbeth: 'no monster'

Ellen played most of the main female parts in Shakespeare's plays at the Lyceum, but one striking omission was Rosalind in As You Like It. Her admirers angrily attributed this to Irving's belief that there was no part in it for him. Ellen was unworried, but in later years her disillusion with her parts at the Lyceum started to grow.

Ellen's performance as Lady Macbeth in 1888 took the controversial line that she was a womanly woman, whose behaviour stemmed from wifely devotion.

Lady Macbeth: 'no monster'

The company returned to London in 1888. Ellen was now at the height of her fame and popularity. If she even walked down the streets of London or other towns in England and Scotland, she was mobbed by delighted crowds. Bernard Shaw believed that every male theatregoer of the last quarter of the century was in love with her. Yet despite this, the problem facing Irving was to find parts for himself and Ellen now that age was a factor.

He was considering *Macbeth* although Ellen tried to dissuade him, aware he was critically condemned the last time he took the part and also worried that she would not be able to identify with Lady Macbeth. She suggested *As You Like It*, which she herself was longing to do, or *King John, Richard II, Julius Caesar* or *The Tempest*. Irving was tempted by the part of Caliban in the latter, but said 'the young lovers are everything, and where are we going to find them?'

He had already set his mind on *Macbeth* so he and Ellen went up to Scotland to get ideas for the scenes, then spent their summer together in Lucerne with Edy and Ted, who joined the party from Germany, and the Comyns Carrs.

Ellen had previously been writing warning letters to Ted: 'Remember, dear, it's your duty to please them, not the Masters' duty to please you!' She also told him that in August of 1888 she was moving from Longridge Road to 22 Barkston Gardens in Earl's Court. 'It's nice, I tell you.' The houses had lawns and trees and colourful window-boxes. Ted gave a graphic picture of

141

Ellen's life then, saying that she spent most of her time upstairs on the second floor in the three-windowed bedroom at the front or the large dressing-room at the back. Once her nightly performance or rehearsal was over, she drove back—with boards put up between the facing seats so she could stretch out and sleep. Once home she had supper, read her letters, put them back into her large chaotic handbag and, usually long after midnight, went to bed.

He remembered her staying there all the next morning until lunch-time. 'She would attend to her correspondence there—sitting up in bed, a board on her knees—read a little, and try to rest after the nervous excitement which theatres and acting (as she acted) entail.'

After lunch she invariably drove out to see a friend or shop. Once, Ted recalled, she was passing Jackson's food shop on Piccadilly when a clerk ran out in the street with a big tray of cheeses and she sliced off tiny samples and ordered her favourite.

The house, he remembered, was always full of women: Edy and her friends, Ellen's friends, the housekeeper, and the female servants who incessantly cleaned. 'Ring at the front-door bell—another woman; ding-a-ling-a-ling—a girl this time.' Ellen's sister Kate once told Bernard Shaw that Ellen could easily learn her parts if she chose, but preferred to scatter her mind before the crowed of adoring girls. Visitors gravitated to the 'parlour room' where there were two pianos and comfortable armchairs. But nevertheless it was, he said, not planned as a society house, but as a working house. 'It was E T's house, and run for her, and for her alone, and this demanded quiet.'

Irving believed that Ellen would be splendid as Lady Macbeth, 'the first time it has been acted for many years', but she herself was anxious and worried about it. However, unlike her experience with Juliet, Irving now understood how she felt, writing to her to say: 'Tonight, if possible, the last act. I want to get these great multitudinous scenes over and then we can attack our scenes... Your sensitiveness is so acute that you must suffer sometimes. You are not like anybody else—you see things with such lightning quickness and unerring instinct that dull fools like myself grow irritable and impatient sometimes. I feel confused when I'm thinking of one thing, and disturbed by another.

142

Always on the move, Ellen left Longridge Road for a house in nearby Barkston Gardens (above, 1888). Hopelessly untidy, she happily filled it with Victorian clutter.

That's all. But I do feel very sorry afterwards when I don't seem to heed what I so much value.'[2] Ellen was to write in the margin of this note, 'How seldom!'

Ellen felt that while they were concentrating on *Macbeth* their partnership worked very well. She was aware that Irving could not have worked with a very strong woman, but knew that she in turn might not have been so successful had her partner been a weaker man 'whose ends were less fine.'

There was a lively discussion in the press as to how Miss Terry would interpret Lady Macbeth. The *St James's Gazette* of 19th December forecast that 'it will be something rather different from that of histrionic tradition.' And indeed Ellen studied the part carefully, including Mrs Siddons's memoranda which agreed with Ellen's conception of Lady Macbeth as 'fair, feminine, perhaps even fragile.' Ellen then discovered that Mrs Siddons actually played the part as a 'triumphant fiend.'

Ellen's own view of Lady Macbeth was that she was a be-blackened woman. In her later lectures on Shakespeare's heroines, she considered her 'a woman of the highest nervous organisation, with a passionate intensity of purpose.' She wrote in the margin besides this remark 'there is more of pity than of terror in her end.' Ellen forcibly argued that Lady Macbeth was no monster, but a 'womanly woman' who is 'a woman in everything...her strength is all nervous force; her ambition is all for her husband. She has been the "dearest partner" of all Macbeth's thoughts and actions; she must needs be the partner of his crime.' In the margin she writes, 'I suppose I can say, "That's just like a woman." She faints when coming into the room, she hears him talking away, talking talking —oh, how he talks.' She comments that Lady Macbeth falls sick of a tortured conscience, writing in the margin 'she dies of remorse.' Then she adds: 'I never yet heard of a murderer dying of remorse.'[3]

She was aware, however, that Irving was not altogether satisfied with her sleepwalking scene. In another note he said,

'The sleeping scene will be beautiful too—the moment you are in it—but Lady M should certainly have the appearance of having got out of bed, to which she is returning when she goes off. The hair to my mind should be wild and disturbed, and the whole appearance as distraught as possible and disordered.[4]

The famous green beetle-wing dress which Ellen wore as Lady Macbeth was designed by Alice Comyns Carr and immortalised in John Singer Sargent's portrait of her. Ellen wrote to Edy in Germany to say, 'The picture of me is nearly finished and I think it magnificent. The green and the blue of the dress is splendid, and the expression as Lady Macbeth holds the crown over her head quite wonderful.'[4] The public queued to see it and Irving, who owned the painting, finally hung it in the Beefsteak Room at the Lyceum.

Alice Comyns Carr also designed a dramatic blood-red cloak for Lady Macbeth to wear after the murder scene. Ellen was pleased when, at the first dress rehearsal, Irving praised its fine splash of colour. Less pleasing, however, was the sight the next evening of

144

Ellen in front of her house at Hawkhurst, Sussex. She loved driving around the countryside and had a passion for buying or renting cottages.

Irving in the cloak. As his consort he thought it right for Ellen to wear a more discreet garment.

Macbeth opened on 29th December 1888. As Irving expected, the audience greeted it enthusiastically: the critics were more ambivalent. They unanimously acclaimed the beauty of the production but were less enthusiastic about the performances by the leading actors. Ellen, said *Truth* magazine, gave 'an aesthetic Burne Jonesy, Grosvenor Gallery version of Lady Macbeth, who roars as gently as any sucking dove.'[5] Irving, many critics felt, was hindered by his physical limitations. Ellen's father wrote telling her not to let the critics interfere with her view of the part. 'I had no opportunity to tell you on Saturday how beautiful you looked …it was a grand performance of a most intellectual concept…my joy was prodigious. Always your loving Daddy.'[6]

Ellen wrote to Edy in Germany to say that the play had been a tremendous success, 'and I am a success, which amazes me, for

Ellen in The Dead Heart *in 1889 with 17-year-old Teddy. She said, 'Here was I in the very noonday of life called upon to play a rather uninteresting mother.' For Teddy's sake, she did.*

never did I think I should be let down so easily. Some people hate me in it; some, Henry among them, think it my best part, and the critics differ, and discuss it hotly, which in itself is my best success of all!…Oh, it's fun, but it's precious hard work for I by no means make her a "gentle, lovable woman" as some of 'em say. That's all pickles. She was nothing of the sort, although she was not a fiend, and did love her husband. I have to what is vulgarly called "sweat at it" each night.'[7]

Macbeth, playing to capacity houses, ran until 29th June 1889. A couple of months before Queen Victoria asked Ellen and Irving to Sandringham to do an extract from *The Bells* and the trial scene from *The Merchant of Venice*. It was the first time the Queen had ever seen theatrical scenes and Irving regarded it as a tribute to the stage.

That summer Ellen went to stay with Edy in Germany while Ted stayed with Irving. He wrote to his mother, sending his best love to 'the dear old frump and to you', and in return received a flood of letters from Ellen telling him not to go to bed later than 11 pm and be careful not to get a chill. Ted was 17 at the time.

Irving reopened the next season in September 1889 with a revival of *The Dead Heart*, a melodrama set against the background of the French revolution. Ellen was disgusted. 'Here I was in the very noonday of life, fresh from Lady Macbeth and still young enough to play Rosalind, suddenly called upon to play a rather uninteresting mother in *The Dead Heart*.'[8] Her only consolation was that Ted successfully played his first role in it. A reviewer in *The Globe*, commenting on his acting in a future part, said he was at his best. 'It is a pity his best is so bad.'

The following summer Ted toured England with the Haviland and Harvey company, receiving anxious letters about his welfare from Ellen. In August, a month before the Lyceum production of *Ravenswood*, he was booked to go to Northampton and Ellen wrote to him to ask him to sketch the town hall, as his father had designed it. 'It, and heaps of other work he did afterwards, shd have made his fortune, but he was very careless of money and wasted it and died very poor—But there was no one like him, none—a man born long before his time—of extraordinary gifts, and of comprehensive genius.'[9]

Ravenswood was a weak version of Walter Scott's novel, *The Bride of Lammermoor*, in which Ted appeared as Ellen's younger brother. It was totally unmemorable, except for Ellen coming off stage one night, after a scene with Irving in which she had to burst into hysterical laughter, to find Irving waiting for her, much put out, to ask why she had finished laughing early. She said she had laughed as usual. 'No you didn't,' said Irving. 'You always say Ha-ha 17 times. You only said it 14 times tonight.'[10] Ellen said she would never be able to act the scene in future without visualising Irving standing there, counting.

Health remained a problem for Ellen. Her letters to friends constantly say that she has been ill—with neuralagia, influenza, headaches, sore throats. In the May of 1891 she fell ill again, though of what is unknown, and Irving wrote to 'My Nell' on 3rd June to say:

'The worst will be over now I hope—but you have had a terrible time.

No one thought—nor did I dream how bad you were. Do pray be careful. Today is just as damp and cheerless as yesterday was dry and bright.

It was better to do the new piece (A Regular Fix) last night wasn't it? I told you it went well—but it's a stop gap and nothing more. Nance with you in it is a genuine attraction and no wonder either, for your acting is very beautiful...

I am anxious to see Ted and hear of you...'[11]

Ellen's disillusion with her parts at the Lyceum continued. *Henry VIII* was staged early January 1892 but she admitted 'I was not keenly interested in it, or in my part.' Edy, back from Germany some two years ago and now 23, played a lady-in-waiting to Ellen's Queen Katherine. Ellen was to write to a friend saying 'Edy walks on in some of our plays and now and then has a line or so given her to speak, but although I never should be surprised if she did something great some day, either as a writer, or an actress or a musician, the fact remains at present a hard fact that she does nothing whatever well!'[12]

In the March of 1892, Ellen's mother Sarah died. When Ellen returned to the theatre after an absence of a few days, she found Irving had thoughtfully filled her dressing room with daffodils 'to make it like sunshine.' The theatre was packed for the run of *Henry VIII*, but the lavish production cost £12,000 and despite its success the season showed a £4,000 loss. Ill-health and ill-luck were now to dog Irving. In November Ellen, now 45, was to play Cordelia in *King Lear*, considering it a most difficult part, 'so little to say, so much to feel.'

By now Ellen had given up her Hampton Court cottage and

As Cordelia in King Lear *in 1892. One critic wrote that she 'seemed to have cast away 10 or 15 years of anxious and harassing life'.*

instead taken over a 17th-century house at the end of a row of cottages in Uxbridge. It was an off-licence and she named it after her understudy, The Audrey Arms. She kept customers away by only offering undrinkable beer.

The following year, 1893, Irving staged *Becket*, in which Ellen had the minimal part of Fair Rosamund. Irving asked Ted, 21 that year, to join the Lyceum company which was to tour America again that autumn, but he wrote to his mother to say he was

Ellen as Fair Rosamund in Tennyson's play, Becket, *staged in 1893.*
Tennyson had died the previous year, never to know the play was an
instantaneous success.

thinking of marrying a young art student, May Gibson. She
wrote back to say his duty to May, himself and his art was 'to
go like a man to America, make some money, for the first time
in your life.' He defied her, turned down the American tour
and married May on 27th March that year. Ellen, writing to
her sister Kate from Chicago on 8th October, said she wrote
to him constantly and heard from him equally frequently. She
admitted she sent home nearly all her money every week, only

keeping back just enough on which to manage.

May's first child was born on 14th April 1894. When the parents and baby came to stay for a week Ellen, prevented from having any say in the child's care, wrote to a friend to admit she was thankful they had left. 'My experience is that it's bitterly disappointing being a Grandmother—and I had thought it would be so lovely …His wife contrives to irritate me more I think than any other person I have ever met with but she's Ted's wife and I'll do my best to keep from spanking her.'[13]

Ellen didn't have to tolerate her too long. Ted's marriage broke up four years later in 1898, though by then he had sired four children. Ellen was furious with him for breaking his marital contract ('Really you are too silly Ted in some things') but still shouldered his financial difficulties. In addition, for the rest of her life, she paid May's alimony.

Ellen was now busy rehearsing the part of Queen Guinevere for Jo Comyns Carr's verse play, *King Arthur*, which opened at the Lyceum on 12th January 1895. A writer for the magazine *Mainly About People* recalled seeing Ellen sprawled out on Hampstead Heath, her hair looking like fibre on a coconut, and holding the play in whichever hand she was not using for gesticulation.

The highlight of the year was on 24th May, when Irving heard that the Queen had conferred a knighthood on him in personal recognition and for his services to art. He drove straight to Ellen to tell her the news. 'The dear fellow deserves any honour, all honours', she said.

When it was announced the next day, a packed house at the Lyceum, where Irving was acting *King Arthur*, gave him a standing ovation. Ellen was delighted, the only shadow on the day being the news that Oscar Wilde had been convicted at the Old Bailey. He had written some sonnets to Ellen and they had exchanged letters, one of which from him began 'Your love is more wonderful even than a crystal caught in bent reeds of gold…'[14] Ellen regarded him with warmth as a friend. A veiled lady thought to be Ellen left some violets and a message of sympathy at his house. Irving did not know Wilde very well, but he was one of the few to send him a message of encouragement on his release.

Ellen, Ellenor, Ellenest

Ellen's letters to Bernard Shaw were a much-needed emotional outlet. She treated him as a father-confessor, poured out all her thoughts to him, discussed theatre matters seriously and deflected or refuted his attacks on Irving. She also asked him, desperately at times, to find work for her and for her

Ellen kept a firm grip on Edy's personal life while she herself was conducting a 'paper courtship' with Bernard Shaw, who wrote exuberantly to his 'Ellen, Ellenor, Ellenest'.

Ellen, Ellenor, Ellenest

To Irving's irritation, Bernard Shaw, the newly appointed critic of the *Saturday Review*, heaped ridicule on *King Arthur*. He considered Ellen's Queen Guinevere a 'heartless waste of exquisite talent', calling her 'a born actress of real women's parts condemned to figure as a mere artist's model in custume plays which, from the woman's point of view, are foolish flatteries written by gentlemen for gentlemen.'[1]

Ellen was rather intrigued by Shaw. She had written to him briefly in 1892 to ask his opinion of a composer-singer friend as Shaw had a reputation as a music critic as well as a socialist orator. Their correspondence revived some three years later and was to last, on and off, for a further 20 years. At one point they were exchanging letters every two or three days. Their letters were intimate, flirtatious, funny, critical, searingly honest and perceptive. Shaw once exuberantly started a letter, 'Ellen Ellen Ellen Ellen Ellen Ellen Ellen Ellen Ellen Ellenor Ellenest Terry.'

Over the years the two deliberately refrained from meeting, both instinctively feeling that to do so would spoil their growing 'paper courtship.' Shaw was also aware a meeting could have engendered a full-scale row, given his constant exasperation with Irving. Irving had no time for new dramatists like Henrik Ibsen and the plays he chose, Shaw balefully considered, wasted Ellen's talent as actress and Irving's as producer.

Shaw was further enraged at the slowness of Irving's movements and speech on stage, which effectively slowed down Ellen. He criticised Ellen for squandering herself too much on other people and interests, citing her disappearance with Godwin. Irving, he pointed out, would never have left the stage for a single night, even to spend it with Helen of Troy.

Ellen was caught in the cultural cross-current between Shaw and Irving and their two worlds. Shaw was a crusader for social reform, women's rights and the destruction of class privilege. He regarded plays like *Olivia* as trash whereas Irving, when once urged by various people to read Ibsen's *The Pretenders*, did so and 'was left staring before him all through the night wondering was he or all his friends stark staring raving mad!' Irving represented the established order of Victorian convention, staging Shakespearian or traditional plays with meticulously planned and beautiful sets.

When the correspondence between Shaw and Ellen re-started in 1895, it was when she was depressed at the poor parts being offered her and aware as she approached her 50th year that there was little future at the Lyceum. Shaw was in a position as drama critic for the *Saturday Review* to express his disgusted views on the Lyceum's programme.

Irving had announced that the 1896 season would open with *Coriolanus*. Down at Winchelsea in August 1895 with Ellen and Edy and friends, he read out loud to them his prepared version and they thought it duller and duller. Ellen told him so but Irving disagreed, then next morning called out to her from his bedroom to say he wouldn't do it. 'Joy, joy', said Ellen. (It would be staged in 1901.) Irving then toyed with the idea of *Julius Caesar*. When Shaw heard of this he promptly wrote to Ellen to say he was further shocked at the news the Lyceum might be putting on some obsolete rubbish like *Julius Caesar*, and castigated the Shakespeare-struck Irving.

On the last day of August 1895, Ellen together with Edy and Irving left for a further tour of Canada and the United States. The company followed on another ship and Ellen seeing how Irving hated meeting them all and, as he said, 'shaking their greasy paws,' considered she had been very useful to him as a buffer. She thought his best assets were 'his patience, his caution, his strong, practical will, and his gentle courtesy. His worst is his being incapable of caring for people, sons, friends, any one, and his lack of enthusiasm for other people's work.'[2]

One of the plays in the itinerary was *Macbeth* in which Margaret (May) Webster, a member of the company along with her husband Ben, played a gentlewoman. She remembered how in New York a tiny lamp flared up and caught Ellen's hair on fire. May deftly put out the sudden flame with her cloak and Ellen later gave her a picture of herself, holding the lamp, on the back of which she had written 'This way to Mrs Gaze's party. Three steps up and fall over your drapery.'

The company travelled down through the southern cities in the winter of 1895. One night, May recalled, as they crossed a flooded river, the water nearly reached the engine fires. Edy rushed to her mother's compartment to see how she was and found her completely dressed, gloves neatly buttoned and tying her veil. 'Edy darling,' she said, 'hurry and dress yourself properly; we shall probably have to swim!'[3]

One of the plays in the tour itinerary was *Godefroi and Yolande*, a one-act play based on Swinburne's poem *The Leper*, by Irving's son, Laurence, which Irving had thought too morbid and insubstantial to stage at the Lyceum. Ellen had persuaded Irving to include it in the American tour as part of a triple bill, under her direction, while Edy devised its scenery, effects and costumes.

May wrote to her sister-in-law from New Orleans to say 'We're rehearsing that filthy leper play every day, takes up all our time, and it's in such a muddle owing to the erratic Nell's stage management.' Ellen was in a state about the lights and May rushed to Loveday, the stage manager, to tell him 'for God's sake get that lime on her or she'll go mad.' She heard a chuckle from the darkness and Irving's voice saying 'Better get it right, Loveday. Don't want her to go mad, y'know. Pity.'[4]

After the arduous trip through the south, the company were relieved to stay a month in Chicago. What happened there revealed Ellen's fierce possessiveness towards Edy, which Edy was later to show over Ellen. May Webster, staying at their hotel, thought Edy brusque, but knowledgeable, almost belligerently talented, passionately devoted to Ellen and with all the problems of an illegitimate daughter of a famous and beautiful actress. Ellen wrote to Shaw only the following year to say 'I wish you'd marry her! (Edy) Nobody else will. (The ninnies are frightened at her!)'

According to May, in Chicago Edy fell passionately in love with a married man, Sidney Valentine. Ellen reacted violently, mercilessly crushing the incipient romance and threatening to send Edy back to England. In May's view Ellen made matters worse by her deliberate flirtation with one of the cast members, the handsome if wooden (and married) Frank Cooper, who was descended from the Kemble theatrical family. 'She would bring him back to supper after the performance and insist Edy should stay up—or get up, if she had not been playing herself that night—in order to chaperone her.'[5] Edy, said May, remained in the company and did as she was told and the episode was never mentioned again.

What is sad and unexpected is that Ellen, who showed immense sympathy and understanding to Irving and her many friends throughout her life, could bring none of these qualities to help her own daughter. She showed no insight into Edy's feelings and acted in an apparently deliberately cruel way. Edy, hurt and upset, rejected her mother and took her meals with the Websters, to Ellen's apparent surprise. Ellen, who would spend weeks studying and trying to understand a character in a play, appeared unable to comprehend her own daughter.

Ellen needed her, needed her devoted love, needed her attention. Anyone who threatened this tie would encounter the full force of Ellen's anger. Yet she seemed unable to disentangle her own feelings about Edy, writing at the time of this episode to Shaw to say 'I've prayed that she might love, but I don't pray for that now. I'll tell you some day when we've time to meet.'

On her return from America, Ellen was told of her father's death. Upset, she plunged into rehearsals for Imogen in *Cymbeline* which opened at the Lyceum on 22nd September 1896. Ben Webster and Ellen's son Ted played the two young princes, speaking the dirge 'Fear no more the heat o' the sun' over Imogen's body, and had the problem of lifting Ellen up when she often went into fits of giggles, accusing them of tickling her. Ellen thought Ted a wonderful actor, but though he inherited her massive charm he was conceited, adolescent in outlook, and generally disliked by the other actors. Ben Webster was once jostled on stage by some

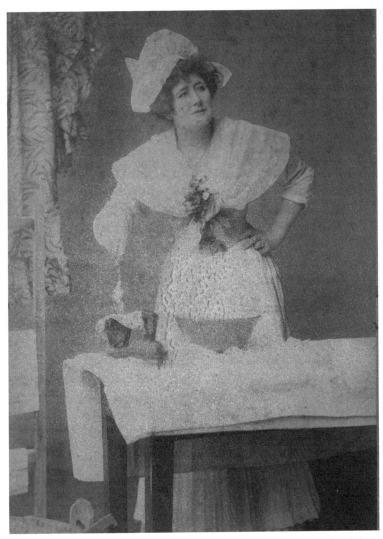

Ellen scored a success in 1897 as Madame Sans-Gêne in the comedy of that name. Her costume varied from that of laundry maid to royal robes.

'soldiers' who apologised when they found out he was not Ted.

Bernard Shaw wrote to Ellen a fortnight before *Cymbeline* opened, heading a penetrating essay of advice on the part, 'The Intelligent Actress's Guide to *Cymbeline*.' This amused Ellen, always pleased to be given a fresh approach to her art. She thanked him, ending that she was in tremors about wearing 'that boy's dress (being fat and nearly 50)'. While exchanging several more letters on the subject, Ellen gave light-hearted descriptions of the cast: 'A lovely voice and never shouts'; 'Shouts, but has a sweet face'; 'Was a parson, so he must be good.'[6]

She believed her part as Imogen to be the only inspired performance she gave in 'these last rather sad years' of the Lyceum, though promptly told Shaw that her peformance was stiff and dull. Shaw kept up his barrage of invective against Irving, telling her he was shocked to hear she was to be cast as the washer-woman in *Madame Sans Gêne* when he had just finished a one-act play (*Man of Destiny*) which would be perfect for her. Ellen read it, told Shaw it was 'delicious' but failed to persuade Irving to stage it.

In writing to Shaw, she discussed theatre matters seriously, deflected or refuted his attacks on Irving, commented on his plays (she criticised the length of the speeches in *Mrs Warren's Profession*) and maintained a lightly flirtatious tone. 'Give my love to every bit of you. Especially the dear old ears. I love them best now, because you made fun of them.'[7]

The frequency of their letters grew in intensity and remained at a peak for the next four or so years. Ellen treated Shaw as a father-confessor, pouring out all her thoughts to him, including her private, often jumbled feelings about Edy:

'Edy looks a tragedy, and is about the most amusing, funniest creature living, a casual wretch. Oh she is odd. Envy was not in the mixture that made her up, nor me…She'll try and go away for a whole month sometimes, and hates it, and always gets into a difficult corner…She's high, she's low. She's a perfect Dear. She loathes emotional people, yet adores me…I heard she said once "Not one minute would I stop with Mother, but that I do just as I like". (She thinks she does but really she does as I like.)'[8]

Ellen was to ask Shaw if he could find an opening for her and though he said that she had a very beautiful voice and was both clever and capable, he thought she was too young for heavy parts. But the following year, 1897, he suggested to Mr and Mrs Charrington, who ran the Independent Theatre Company, that they consider her for a part in *Candida* and *The Doll's House*. As a result, Edy joined the company. Although she admired Irving as an actor, like Shaw she had little time for the Lyceum style of production or plays and found the Independent Theatre, which aimed at producing plays of 'literary and artistic rather than commercial value' an intellectual outlet. She could act intelligent parts in intelligent plays but her contradictory personality, at once too aggressive and too shy, prevented her success.

Ellen was pleased at her daughter's new direction, though upset when a friend told her that 'If Edy stays long with the Independent Theatre Company she will get dull, heavy, conceited, frowsy, trollopy, and dirty! In fact will look moth-eaten! And no one will see her act, because nobody goes to their Theatre.' She told Shaw 'That's lively news for Edy's Mama, who is missing her all the while, and for you who have a play there.'[9]

Ellen was quick to try and help Edy professionally, but she failed to provide a comforting shoulder, or sympathy and understanding if Edy was in personal distress. There were no sexual confidences or understanding. From childhood, Edy had to struggle to get attention as her mother was tired through overwork and was invariably surrounded by other people. Ellen was affectionate and proud of her, but she was a strong, dominating woman and tried with the best will in the world to manage her daughter's life. Mother knows best.

Edy in turn, to avoid being swamped, developed an aggressive, acerbic personality. She achieved self-reliance but at a cost. Referring to this in the edited version of Ellen's memoirs, Christopher St John commented, 'Edy was unsympathetic to her mother in her early years because she was developing her powers of resistance to this domestic tornado. Edy finally got the upper hand, and so lost her fear of her mother, and with it her hatred of her. The word is a hard one, but children do really hate their parents in their struggle for independence.'[10]

The more Ellen became an icon, admired and sought after by everyone, the more private Edy became. As both her children grew up Ellen, often from America, deluged them with loving letters and advice. She was less able to snatch the time to talk to them. Edy had learned over the years to manage her own emotions and not to depend on a frequently absent mother. She had never formed the habit of confiding in Ellen, and after Ellen's unsympathetic behaviour over the American she had fallen for, she was unlikely to try.

161

Ellen as Sylvia Winford in The Medicine Man *in 1898. She did what she could to secure the play's success but it failed dismally.*

Ellen's deteriorating eyesight plagued her during *Cymbeline*, she was not well and, worse, had no parts worthy of her ability in the next few plays: *Madame Sans-Gene* (1897), *Peter the Great* and *The Medicine Man* (1898). Of her part in *The Medicine Man* she said that short as it was, she still felt she couldn't cut too much of it. Shaw told her he was grinding his teeth at her wasting her life on such parts and he simply couldn't understand Irving's policy. He and Irving had fallen out over a review of Shaw's and Ellen's hopes of Irving staging Shaw's *The Man of Destiny* were dashed.

Ellen's relationship with Irving was in decline. She was to say to Shaw, 'H and I are out!…I don't agree with him about you, and he knows it'; and in speaking of the late 1890s, Ellen told Marguerite Steen: 'He began to get tired of me and to pay attention to other women. I wasn't jealous, but I said, "I love and adore you, and while you wanted it everything that was mine was yours. But when you ceased to want it—No".'[11] She told Shaw that 'Henry is so nice to me lately that I'm convinced he has a new "flame"', then asked him in the February of 1898, who on earth was 'Mrs A'?

Mrs A was in fact a Mrs Aria, a well-known London journalist, whose acquaintance with Irving had begun the previous summer. Shaw diplomatically told Ellen she was 'a good sort.' Irving had met her at a supper party and had liked her intelligence and dry humour. They initially went on carriage drives together and the close friendship that developed lasted for years. He never mentioned her to Ellen, but to her it signalled the end of their relationship. Marguerite Steen said in later years she gave Ellen a biography of Irving by Mrs Aria and Ellen had laid it aside saying, 'Thank you, my dear…Henry left me for Mrs Aria.'

Ellen's own behaviour was being equally gossiped about. She had, perhaps deliberately in view of Irving's defection, revived her partiality for the Lyceum company actor, Frank Cooper, a flirtation she had started in America when Edy had been smitten by Sidney Valentine. Ben Webster, who shared Cooper's lodgings, thought Ellen was degrading herself. She infuriated Irving by calling him Frank throughout supper one evening. She wrote light-heartedly to her friend Bertha Bramley later that year to say, 'No—I fear I can't snap up Frank Cooper (!) and marry him, for he happens to have a wife—and she's nice too—so he can't "cut her throat with a bar of soap".'[12]

Ellen was more worried about Edy at the time, as she was proposing to go on a South African tour, and begged Shaw to find her a London engagement. 'It is so bad for her to be far from me for a long time.' Edy obviously did not feel the same. The tour, however, never materialised. Ellen admitted to Shaw in the

November of 1897 that when Edy was away, Ted busy with his family and Irving single-mindedly involved with his work, she felt lonely:

'But the feeling of loneliness (for that's what it is, loneliness mixed up with jealousy, ugh! detestably!) passes directly Edy turns up. I think she is the only one I was ever jealous about. Folk think she cares for me. I don't. I never plague her with my love, but oh, how she cuts my heart to ribbons sometimes, and very likely she doesn't intend to be unkind!'[13]

Her correspondence with Shaw was gradually dwindling. A contributing factor could have been his marriage in 1898, lessening his reliance on Ellen for affection and intimate exchange of thoughts.

During the following few years the vogue of the Lyceum declined, exacerbated by a disastrous fire in 1898 which destroyed 260 elaborate scenic sets. Under-insured, they were irreplaceable. The Lyceum's finances were by now desperate and when a syndicate approached Irving offering to float a public company which would take all financial responsibility in return for taking over his interests in the Lyceum for the remaining eight years' lease, Irving agreed and surrendered his independence. Under the terms Irving was to give at least 100 performances a year, as well as guaranteeing to play on tour for at least four months a year. ('Every season both of us to play at the Lyceum from April till July,' said Ellen crossly.) In 1898 The Lyceum became The Lyceum Limited Liability Company.

The strain told. Irving became seriously ill at the end of that year and was laid up for months at Bournemouth. Ellen thought it had changed him. 'He is stouter, very grey, sly-looking, and more cautious than ever. Bother!'[14] She admitted feeling a strange mixture of contempt, affection and admiration for him. He asked her to visit him at Bournemouth in January 1899, where he explained that he was financially ruined and that a syndicate was taking over the Lyceum. His plans were to take a very small company around the provinces. Ellen asked where she came in. He said that for the present, she could do as she liked. It stunned her. 'Then I have in plain terms what Ted would call "the dirty kick out"?' she said.[15]

After what Ellen called the 'farcical Lyceum syndicate' took over the theatre, in the April of 1899 she played 'a wretched part' in *Robespierre*. 'The idea that I deserted the sinking ship is rubbish,' she said. She still worked intensely at rehearsals, refusing a luncheon date with a friend saying, 'it's 'ammer, 'ammer, 'ammer on the 'ard 'igh road'. However, the memorable partnership between her and Irving was disintegrating. Irving wanted her to continue acting with him, and she would have done so happily had he been able to offer her any reasonable parts. As it was, she knew she would either have to accept parts from other managements or go into management on her own.

She told Shaw that though she was engaged to tour America that winter, 'and go I will, must!' when she came back, if she was offered a fairly good part at the Lyceum she would play it, but if it was like 'the kind of thing I did (or didn't) in *Peter the Great*, *Medicine Man* or *Robespierre* I shall "refuse to act" (for the first time in my life) and give it all up...I should never say good-bye. Just leave off.'[16]

Ellen constantly tried to interest Irving in Shaw's plays. She gave him a copy of *Caesar and Cleopatra* to read, considering the part of Caesar ideal for him, but he rejected it and refused to give his reasons. She told Shaw she was now convinced that Irving would never produce anything of his. Irving remained resistant to 'the new drama,' preferring melodramas, comfortable comedies or the bedrock of Shakespeare to plays written by, to his mind, 'rebels' against the prevailing social conventions.

That same summer of 1899, Shaw gave Ellen a copy of his play, *Captain Brassbound's Conversion* but was greatly disappointed with her reaction, which was 'I couldn't do this one, and I believe it would never do for the stage.' She disliked the character of Lady Cicely Waynflete, apparently unaware it was based on her. Shaw replied, naturally enough, that Lady Cicely fitted her like a glove. Ellen tried to slip it past Irving's guard by asking him to read it but not telling him it was by Shaw. He still rejected it, refusing to see the writing on the theatrical wall.

While Ellen was touring America with Irving in 1899,
Edy moved into the flat of a friend, Chris St John.
The two women delightedly experimented with their
independence, wearing striking hats swathed in cocks'
feathers and dining with artists, painters and actresses.
Ellen considered Chris had 'stolen' Edy away.

Edy: love takes all

Ellen muffled against the cold on her way to rehearsal in Philadelphia during a 1901 tour. She found such tours exhausting but needed the money to support her children and other dependents.

Edy: love takes all

The year 1899 was a crucial landmark in Edy's life. Ellen received a poem from one of her young women worshippers called Christabel Marshall and in her usual casual way invited her along to the theatre during a suburban tour. Arriving in a red coat and small black three-cornered hat, she was promptly handed over to Edy for safekeeping. Edy, mending a glove, shook hands while holding the needle, and accidentally pricked Chris. 'Cupid's dart', Chris was to say, 'for I loved Edy from that moment.'

The feeling was to become mutual, although Edy was initially antagonistic, as her mother's women adorers were apt to be a nuisance. Chris went back to a midnight meal with them at Barkston Gardens and Edy admitted she fitted in and didn't seem like a stranger.

Edy and Chris met for lunch the next day. Chris was secretary to Lady Randolph Churchill at the time and a budding writer, while Edy was making some of the costumes for Irving's production of *Robespierre*. There are countless descriptions of Ellen but few of Edy. Chris recalled her as she was then:

'She had not yet reached her 30th birthday, but in her dark hair, nearer black than brown, there was already one white lock. Her brown eyes, set wide apart, were perhaps the most beautiful feature of her face. The nose was rather too long, though its upward tilt deceived one about that. The straight lips were a fault in her mouth, which otherwise was very like her mother's. She had a lovely slender figure in these days, and looked taller than

Ellen's relationship with her daughter was mutually loving but possessive.
They had a strong emotional tie and resented the 'intrusion' of rivals.

she was (about 5ft.8in.) owing to her elevation. Her carriage was perfect in its grace.'[1]

Edy decided to move in with Chris during her mother's tour of America with Irving in the October of 1899 and the two took a Queen Anne house in Smith Square, Westminster, where, Chris admitted, they lived recklessly beyond their means for six years. Irene Cooper Willis, a mutual friend, gave a graphic description of their buoyant life together there:

'The atmosphere was quite undomestic, the telephone rang incessantly, Edy and Chris shouted commands from different headquarters, and all the things that I had been brought up to believe should be done first, bed-making, dusting and washing up, were done last or, quite likely, not done at all.'[2]

Ellen welcomed the idea of the two of them sharing a place while she was away. Meanwhile, she was preparing for the Lyceum company's American tour that winter of 1899. Once there they received strong public support, but Ellen noted critically that Irving, on stage, now concentrated on details rather than great emotional effects. She still enjoyed being in America, telling Shaw with amusement about a society column's announcement that 'Mrs Otis will hold a *Welsh Rarebit* in honor of her niece.'

But it was the Boer war in South Africa, started over the treatment of British subjects in the Transvaal, that was currently stirring up her emotions and she wrote from America to Shaw on 28th January 1900 to say 'The war—and the disgrace of it (Beef-headed Buller's doings)—this is the only subject which excites me and makes me want to kill, Kill, KILL!'[3] In the May of that year, Ted and his friend, the gifted composer Martin Shaw, produced Purcell's *Dido and* Aeneas. Midway through the last performance news came through that Mafeking had been relieved and half the audience rushed out to buy a paper.

Ellen's own plans at the time were confused. While in America she had discussed with Irving the ending of their professional partnership. On her return to London in the June of 1900, her reaction to playing *Olivia* yet again was 'Too bad! Everyone, but H., is about half my age. I'm angry at having to do it, but patience!'[4] Ellen was now 52 and had natural worries about her future.

She suggested to Irving that after one more season at the Lyceum she should make a two-year farewell tour and retire on the proceeds. Then Irving suggested they did an autumn American tour that same year, to which Ellen, needing the immediate money, agreed. She apologetically asked Shaw to cast *Captain Brassbound's Conversion* without her, writing to say 'I appear to be of strange use to H, and I have always thought to be useful, really useful, to any one person is rather fine and satisfactory.'[5] Ellen had been maddening Shaw by her procrastination over this play and he wrote to her on 9th February 1900 to agree they should 'cry off' from it and add, waspishly, that he knew she would never be able to detach herself from the Lyceum. Irving then decided against the tour and Ellen wrote to Shaw complaining about folk 'who wont play fair' and that she was 'deeply furious (inwardly) that all my desire for *Brassbound* is all of no use.'

She was also faced with Edy's decision to stay on living with Chris. Chris said that she later accused her of having enticed Edy from their home in Barkston Gardens and had come between mother and daughter. Certainly Ellen had taken Edy's constant presence for granted and assumed she would always stay looking after her. She might adore Ted but it was Edy on whom she depended.

Edy and Chris delightedly experimented with their independence. The two women lightheartedly wore striking hats swathed in cocks' feathers, and constantly lunched and dined at the Gourmet Restaurant with artists, painters and actresses. Edy, living away from home for the first time, had her first taste of freedom and loved it.

Chris, now writing for a living, wrote an anonymous fictional autobiography in 1915, calling it *Hungerheart* in the best tradition of melodramatic romance. She disguised all the names and wrote of Louise's (Ellen's) jealousy when she discovered her daughter was not coming back to live with her. She described what her daughter, Sally (Edy) said about this:

'You don't know mother. She wants me because I have gone away. When I lived at home I hardly ever saw her...partly because she was never there and partly because she can never bear to be with any one for long at a time. Please don't think I mean she doesn't love me. Of course she does—tremendously; at the same time she has all sorts of ideas and sentiments that she doesn't wish realised. One of them is my living with her and looking after her. No one can look after my mother.'[6]

This could have been based on what Edy told her. But Chris, a plain woman with the added disadvantage of a speech impediment, had never been seriously involved before and may have dramatised the situation. For instance, although a legitimate daughter of a Victorian novelist, she claimed to be the offspring of a romantic affair.

The letters which Ellen wrote to Edy shortly after her return from America show no hint of any strained relations. Ellen often casually mentions Chris (who changed her name from Christabel Marshall to Christopher St John on converting to Catholicism), such as asking how her story for the *Daily Mail* was getting on. One letter to Edy thanks them both for their birthday presents: 'The bag was lovely and as for the head wrap—it makes me long to go out to "a damned party in a parlour." How beautifully it was done…Thank you my minx. Just the sort of present I like. Chris was naughty (but nice) to spend her money on me. You must make her understand I don't very much like to have presents—and costly ones—"rich gifts" positively pain me—I can't tell her this, but you will know how—I wouldn't hurt her for the world.'[7]

Edy was re-playing the part of Prossy in *Candide* for the Stage Society that July, but was also developing her abilities as a theatrical costumier. Ellen told Shaw that Edy's work was 'crowds of dresses at nothing a piece and all excellent.' Without an allowance from her mother, Edy could not have continued. Rarely did Ted or Edy achieve economic independence from Ellen: like fledgings in the nest, they always looked on her as their provider. Ted in particular was constantly bludgeoning her for money and proud though Ellen was of him, she often became furious. 'Your bent towards cleverness does not lie in the management of money', she snapped.

Ellen was recuperating from exhaustion at Aix-Les-Bains in the September of 1900, writing to a friend complaining the cure was too violent and that she was getting her strength together before leaving with Irving on a tour round Britain next month. While in Newcastle that November she was still dithering about possibly playing Lady Cicely Waynflete in *Captain Brassbound's Conversion*, but told Shaw she now had her hands full as Irving was ill. She was worried by his obvious frailty on his recovery, but found him cold and unresponsive. Unwell herself, she wrote to Shaw to say:

'Ah, I feel so certain Henry just hates me! I can only guess at it, for he is exactly the same sweet-mannered person he was when "I felt so certain" Henry loved me! We have not met for years now, except before other people, where my conduct exactly matches his of course. All my own fault. It is I am changed, not he. It's all right, but it has squeezed me up dreadfully…if I were not a worm I'd take my illness as an excuse to outsiders and leave all theatres, Henry,

The farmhouse, Smallhythe Place. Ellen first saw it when driving around Kent with Irving and decided immediately that was where she wanted to live and die.

"and such like trash," behind me and go and live on my farm.'[8]

Ellen had bought this 'farm', a timbered 16th-century farmhouse, at Smallhythe in Kent, two months previously and although essentially a city person she regarded her farmhouse like her previous cottages as a retreat from the world and spent much of her future life there. She had seen it some years previously, when driving in a pony-trap with Irving around the marshlands between Rye and Tenterden, and was immediately attracted to it. She asked an old shepherd living there if it was a nice house: 'No', he said.

Undeterred she asked him to tell her if it came up for sale and in 1900 received an unsigned postcard saying, 'House for sale.'

Edy and Chris went down to look at it and despite rooms being full of fleeces were immediately enthusiastic, so Ellen bought it. The property included two adjacent cottages and a large barn and Ellen let Edy and Chris live in one of the cottages called the Priest's House. Ellen was thrilled, writing to a friend to say, 'Do you know I am a landed proprietor—I have an acre of ground and a cottage. My very own and freehold.'

Shaw had relinquished the idea of Ellen ever appearing in *Captain Brassbound's Conversion* but had managed to get it produced by the Stage Society. Its first performance was on 16th December 1900. Despite her tour, Ellen managed to get to it and she and Shaw met there for the first time. This was followed, coincidentally, by a 15-month gap in their correspondence and Ellen was to remark, 'They say you could not bear me, when we met, that one time, under the stage.' Over the next 20 years they only averaged about three letters a year.

On 22nd January 1901 the streets of London were draped in mourning crepe in memory of Queen Victoria who had died that day. By inviting Irving and Ellen and members of the company to give theatrical excerpts at her various homes and palaces, the Queen had helped raise the status of the stage.

Just as her reign had seemed to go on for ever, so had the supremacy of the Lyceum in London's theatre world. But now her death was echoed by changes in the theatrical scene. When Ellen and Irving had begun their partnership over 20 years before in 1878, there were only three main theatres with permanent companies. But new playwrights like Arthur Pinero, Oscar Wilde, Bernard Shaw, J M Barrie and Henry Arthur Jones had attracted public interest and had made the Lyceum productions look dated.

There were now new theatres and new managers like Charles Wyndham at the Criterion Theatre and Herbert Beerbohm Tree at Her Majesty's—who was regarded as Irving's Shakespearean successor. And there were new forms of entertainment like the musical plays staged by George Edwardes, which mixed light comedy and musical numbers.

Ellen was still very popular, as evidenced by a letter she wrote to her sister on 20th March 1901 to thank her for her birthday greetings. In it she complained that the crowds of people who sent her letters, telegrams, cards, parcels and even Valentines got worse and worse: 'folk I never saw and never wish to see…I had only less than 300 by three.' She said that Irving was fairly well though she dreaded the effect of rehearsals of *Coriolanus* on him 'such a part, the length, the exertion!! As for Volumnia—a fine character, but "not in my line".' She asked Kate if she could find a tenant for her Winchelsea cottage for £150 a year and wished she had come to the end of the lease for Barkston Gardens, as she was now rehearsing from the rented Vine Cottage, in Kingston Vale. Ellen had a positive mania for renting or buying cottages, at one stage having three.

Ellen's Volumnia in *Coriolanus* was her last part at the Lyceum. It opened on 15th April 1901 and was a dull affair. Ellen received polite notices saying she was 'a stately figure'.

Depressed, she left with Irving on their last tour of America together. Irving was now 63, Ellen 53, and the seven-month tour proved exhausting. But it earned Ellen £300 a week and she needed the money to support the careers of both Edy and Ted as well as other dependents.

She wrote a shocked letter to her sister from Philadelphia on 26th November 1901, after hearing the death of Kate's husband, Lewis. It was loving, sympathetic and down to earth. 'My heart aches for you—only one comfort in all the misery, that death is not the worst that can befall.' To have one's dearest prove unworthy of one's love and honour, said Ellen, was 'surely the very beyond beyond of hopeless misery' while Kate could always remember Lewis as 'so sweet and beautiful a character.'[10]

On returning from America in March 1902, they found that the London County Council was insisting on new fire regulations which would cost the Lyceum £20,000 and effectively bankrupt it. Irving decided to go ahead and stage *Faust*, but Ellen was too old to play Marguerite and with relief accepted an offer from Herbert Tree to play Mrs Page in a rumbustious production of *The Merry Wives of Windsor*. She told Shaw she was going to 'fool about as Mistress Page' for a month or so and indeed did so, putting a pin one night in Falstaff's padding and gleefully watching it collapse.

That June was the coronation of Edward VII and though

After the Lyceum management went bankrupt, Ellen formed her own company in 1903 and presented Ibsen's The Vikings at Helgeland, *playing Hjördis the warrior queen on a set designed by Ted.*

it was postponed owing to his illness, the reception Irving planned at the Lyceum went ahead. It was an Arabian Nights extravaganza, with the stage hung in crimson velvet and a procession of Eastern highnesses in blazing jewelled turbans. It was a glittering end of an era.

A matinee of *The Merchant of Venice*, with Ellen as Portia and

Irving as Shylock, ended the season on 19th July 1902. After their last curtain call, she said to him, 'I shall never be in this theatre again. I feel it…I know it.' She was quite right: the Lyceum went into liquidation within a few months. 'Night's candles are burnt out.'

Irving, indefatigable, now planned to produce *Dante* by Sardou. His intention was to stage it first at the Theatre Royal, Drury Lane in April 1903 and then take it to America. He offered Ellen a large sum of money to take part in the America production, but seeing no viable part in it for herself, she refused. Writing to Shaw on 10th December 1902, she says: 'Henry is pretending he is not furious with me, and that makes me feel a guilty wretch for refusing to speak a few lines in his old Dante.'[11] She and Irving never acted together again.

Although Ellen had told Shaw she did not want to risk her savings, the prop of her old age, by going into management with a less than a cast-iron successful play, she promptly did so by hiring the Imperial Theatre for a season and putting on Ibsen's *The Vikings of Helgeland*, a tragedy based on an Icelandic saga. It was a deliberate move to help her children and was produced by Ted and costumed by Edy. Ellen, rather uncomfortably, played Hjördis a fierce warrior queen. On the first night, in the third act, she admitted 'I forgot most of my words and the whole thing went to pieces.'

The public was not attracted by Ellen as a Viking queen, or by Ted's stage settings, though the artist William Rothenstein wrote: 'so beautifully was the play staged, so nobly were the figures grouped in scene after scene that I felt something important had happened to the English stage.'[12] Ellen agreed, saying 'I hope it will be remembered, when I am spoken of after my death as a "Victorian" actress, lacking in enterprise, an actress belonging to the "old school" that I produced a spectacular play of Ibsen's in a manner which possibly anticipated the scenic ideas of the future by a century.'[13]

The play was unpopular and a financial failure. Under her management Ted then produced *Much Ado about Nothing*, and Shaw, calling the play *Much Adoodle-do*, admitted that nothing quite like it had been done before. But it, too, failed to raise public

178

A serene-looking Ellen in 1903. But Henry Irving commented that 'She has been absolutely under the influence and spell of her two children, who have launched her on a sea of troubles'.

interest. Ted could find no backers for future plays and decided to leave England and 'get along to Germany and to Russia and other lands where my notions were regarded without prejudice, and progress was preferred to argumentative retrogression.'[14]

He attributed the failure of his productions to his mother, criticising her for her lack of strength as an actor manager, due to her long-term reliance on Irving, and also to Edy because of an 'obstructionist' in her costume department who would flare up 'and anathematise me and all the male members of the company.' He decided with disgust the woman was 'not to be held entirely responsible for her devilry—for she had become one of the suffragettes.'[15]

Ted, who ultimately fathered ten children, six of whom were illegitimate, was hardly a natural supporter of women's suffrage. Women, he thought, should be content with ministering unto men, as can be seen by his attitude to the dancer Isadora Duncan with whom he later lived. He asked her why she wanted to go on the stage and wave her arms about: 'Why don't you stay at home and sharpen my pencils?'

As Martin Shaw was the composer for *The Vikings of Helgeland* he had naturally worked alongside Edy. Ted wrote in his diary:

'About this time (1903) my friend Martin Shaw seems to have proposed to my sister Edy. E T was greatly disturbed and came to see me about it, as though it was any of my business. She said it was to be prevented and I must help her to prevent it. Well, all I could do was to do nothing except agree dutifully with E T—but the matter seems to have been pretty soon forgotten. For they did not elope and real lovers always do that if any obstruction is encountered. So E T was right after all.'[16]

Ted may have favoured elopement himself and, like his parents, practised what he preached, but the trauma of the Martin Shaw episode was far greater than he appreciated. Ellen, if what Ted said was to be believed, apparently did not think the couple were in love. But she was wildly and emotionally against the marriage, despite Martin Shaw's obvious abilities. Admittedly, he had a disfiguring birthmark on his face but if Edy did not care about this, why should Ellen? Edy had already left Ellen to live with Chris, so it was not as if Ellen feared losing her. She and Chris, however, were still very much part of Ellen's life. Martin was a man and, in Ellen's view, could remove Edy from her jurisdiction.

Ellen wrote an emotional, self-regarding letter to Ted at this time which showed she was angry enough to ally herself with Chris but failed to explain why she was so against the relationship:

'Edy there tonight at the play with the Hildermans...and crew you introduced to her—oh, I feel so wild with you when I see

180

her with them. Poor Chris seems to be having an awful time of it...They all and others went round to Smith Square afterwards. I took Chris round there for they had left her behind at the theatre...M S was not there—anyway I suppose I want you to tell me what there is against him except his misfortunate personal appearance, his poverty. The Hildermans are backing E up and saying "How fine" etc—Wait!—Poor Edy is absolutely naughty to me...her attitude to me I mean—'m sick at heart and cry my eyes out all through the night—I don't think the affair will come off somehow—with no gilt on the gingerbread they will get sick of each other I believe—oh I am just mad with Edy this moment.'[17]

Chris, in her highly-charged novel, *Hungerheart*, also emphasised Ellen's dislike of Martin and equally failed to explain this:

'I found out that Louise (Ellen) hated him as much as I did. This gave me hope, a hope of which I was ashamed. As Robin (Martin Shaw) had no money, and Sally (Edy) was dependent on her mother, they could hardly leave Louise out of their reckoning. Would Louise stop Sally's allowance if they married? This seemed to me unlikely, but I thought it quite likely that she would reduce it.'[18]

Her mother's attitude must have been pressure enough on Edy, but worse was to come. Chris, horrified by even the possibility that Edy might be leaving her to marry Martin, promptly took an overdose. Her description of the event in *Hungerheart* was all an avid reader of melodrama could want:

'"Yes I care for him," said Sally. "I want to marry him." "That deformity," I cried..."behind my hot forehead my brain felt like ice." I remembered clearly a bottle of cocaine lotion in the bathroom, which had been prescribed for my ear-ache. I went in and drank it without a moment's hesitation.'[19]

The overdose was serious. Chris nearly died and was nursed back to health by Edy. Edy nevertheless must have realised this was emotional blackmail on Chris's part and continued to see Martin. However, nothing came of the relationship: the exhausting emotional reaction may have been too much for both of them. It led to Edy's estrangement from her brother Ted, who was unable to understand how Edy could let herself be browbeaten into leaving Martin. Ellen wrote to him in the December of 1903 to

Attired in an eye-catching Edwardian hat in 1903, Ellen looks more like a society beauty than a working actress. Postcards of her were eagerly sought.

say: 'You and Edy quarrelling has finished me nearly…and shown me we are all standing on the brink of a height from which we shall assuredly topple and be useless any of us to help the other —unless something is done at once to avert the catastrophe.'[20]

She did not seem to realise that she herself had certainly

failed to help Edy. Chris, writing of the episode years later, said that her friendship with Edy at that point 'came near to being a tragedy. Of that Edy never spoke in after years. I think our life together subsequently was all the happier, because we did not break open the grave of a thing past which had threatened to separate us.'[21]

The affair calls into question Edy's own sexual orientation. Marguerite Steen wrote of her that 'she, the ardent feminist, had not sufficient of the feminine in her to rouse the "keen interest in the manly breast" described by Charles Reade. Emotionally and artistically, she was more interested in, and interesting to, her own sex than to the male.'[22] Possibly Edy was bisexual: it is hard otherwise to explain why despite her relationship with Chris, she was still considering marriage with Martin Shaw.

Chris's orientation, on the other hand, is quite clear: on one occasion she spent a night with Vita Sackville-West, commented on in Vita's *Love Journal*. In *Hungerheart* she portrays herself as a congenital lesbian, though says of Sally (Edy) that she liked men 'if they behaved well.' She implies that 'Sally' was sexually reserved and that their physical contact was confined to hand-holding. However, this was a fictional autobiography and it is impossible to disentangle fact from fiction.

Ellen would have been quite uncaring about Edy's relationship with Chris, as long as Edy remained part of her own life. She never gave a hint of Edy's relationship with Chris, not even in her extraordinarily frank letters to Shaw. But any written evidence of Edy and Chris's relationship is lost: letters were deliberately destroyed, if not by Ellen, then by Edy after Ellen's death, and by Chris after Edy's death. Edy never confided in Ellen about her close relationships, being fully aware of the resentment this provoked.

Irving, who left alone to tour America in the winter of 1903 wrote to his friend William Winter to say 'it will be strange and somewhat sad without Nell, but 'twas not to be and I shall not attempt to tell you anything 'til we meet—Poor dear, she has been absolutely under the influence and spell of her two children—who have launched her on a sea of troubles.'[23]

183

London was to celebrate Ellen's stage jubilee in the June of 1906 with a star matinee at Drury Lane. Those appearing included Caruso and Mrs Patrick Campbell and music hall players included Mr Seymour Hicks and all the Bath Buns. However, Ellen, now nearly 60, was having to come to terms with a dwindling career.

The third marriage

In 1904 Ellen took the lead part in J M Barrie's play Alice-sit-by-the-Fire, *with the young A E Matthews and C Aubrey Smith.*

The third marriage

After Irving returned from America in the spring of 1904 he began touring England but he had to stop after his health broke down. Ellen, hearing this, went to see him. They were alone for the first time for several years and she thought he looked 'like some beautiful grey tree she had seen in the Savannah.' Irving welcomed her, saying 'Two Queens have been kind to me this morning. Queen Alexandra telegraphed to say how sorry she was I was ill, and now you.' She asked how he would like the end to come. 'Like that', he said, snapping his fingers.[1]

In the summer of 1904 Shaw asked Ellen yet again to play Cicely in *Captain Brassbound's Conversion* as the Royal Court Theatre was willing to stage his plays. She replied from her farmhouse at Smallhythe refusing. She explained that 'having lost all the money I had' she had to go on a provincial tour from August to December 'else it would have been pleasant to me to have played Cicely for a week for nothing.'

She added that Edy was down there with her. They had obviously made it up for Ellen said: 'she is my right hand, and still growing to be my left hand, and happy as a sandboy all the while. I fear to be too happy in her—I try to be very quiet with it all. She has a cottage of her own here and we visit each other every day!'[2] During the forthcoming tour, Edy acted as stage director. With her costumier workshop in Henrietta Street, Covent Garden, foundering, her main interest now was producing pageants and plays.

Shaw later said unkindly that Ted had become the most famous producer in Europe by not producing anything, while Edy remained the most obscure by producing everything. In fact Ted collected accolades abroad for productions like *Venice Preserved* (1905) in Berlin; *Rosmersholm* (1906) for Eleonora Duse in Florence, and *Hamlet* (1912) at the Moscow Arts Theatre. But the begging letters to Ellen continued.

Shaw wrote in July, with irritation, to say he'd heard she'd got J M Barrie to write a new play for her. 'Very well. VERY well.'

Ellen replied from 215 King's Road, Chelsea, to where she had moved from Barkston Gardens. It was a small early Georgian panelled house and she was to live there until 1921. One advantage ws its nearness to the Chelsea Palace, where Ellen went to listen to Marie Lloyd. The music hall singer used to insist that Ellen went with her between performances 'to have one' at the Six Bells inn, opposite, which Ellen very willingly did.

The Barrie play, *Alice-sit-by-the-Fire*, began on 5th April 1905 at the Duke of York Theatre in London. While acting in it, Ellen heard of Irving's death on 13th October and wrote in her diary, 'Henry died today—"and now there is nothing left remarkable beneath the visiting moon"—Cleopatra.' The following night, when she came to the lines 'It's summer done, autumn begun…I had a beautiful husband once…black as raven was his hair…' she broke down and the curtain was lowered.[3] Irving was buried in Westminster Abbey on 20th October, against the wishes of the Dean's sister who protested no actor should be allowed in Poet's Corner. Flags were hung at half-mast throughout the country and the Lyceum was draped in black crepe. Ellen, at the ceremony, thought how much Irving would have enjoyed producing it.

Ellen's life went on. A major preoccupation was her farmhouse and reams of letters went to and fro, with Ellen issuing practical instructions, often for the number of friends she sent down to stay: 'Make sure plenty of lamps are in good working order, that a newspaper or two is in the house, that the fires don't smoke and that the sheets are aired, also the Chafing-Dish ready and eggs and butter on the table.[4]

She showed herself a careful housekeeper: 'You must get a tin of Bluebell for the Pewter—it is expensive, 6d a tin—but very little is used on a little bit of flannel it is splendid. I liked what you

Ellen, seen here with her friend Pauline Chase in 1905, still liked driving in a pony and trap, but motor cars were becoming the rage.

told me about yr airing the beds and putting the blankets in the warm linen cupboard. You will soon get the floors right with the beeswax and turpentine and then you can keep them in order.' Another letter to the farm manager's wife, Clara, said: 'Oh Clara, think of yr not having moved the cushions of that sofa all this time!!!!! Miss Edy is at Bath for her rheumatism—I went there on Sunday last and found her better.'

Ellen may have captivated everyone with her charm, but she could issue orders like a serjeant major: 'Please order in three more tons of coal—use it carefully. Put the pump right'; 'Look again for knee caps (elastic).' She was quick to defray household expenses at her Kings Road house by having a weekly stream of garden

Ellen was nervous and ill-at-ease as Lady Cicely in Shaw's play, Captain Brassbound's Conversion, *which opened at the Court Theatre in 1906.*

produce sent up to her from the Kent house, although Clara was more often rebuked than complimented: 'The last flowers you sent me Clara were dead, withered. The box you sent them in was very heavy, let it be lighter next time. And you sent no lettuce last time'; 'To make the package lighter, I think you should shell the peas before sending them up to town.'

After years of shilly-shallying, Ellen finally accepted the part of Lady Cicely in *Captain Brassbound's Convention* at the Court Theatre on 20th March 1906. She was not at ease in the part and

Max Beerbohm, writing of it, said her nervousness was very apparent. Ellen was conscious that Shaw was disappointed in her interpretation.

She took a few days' break at her farmhouse in Smallhythe, writing in advance to the farm manager's wife to say: 'If I'm well enough and the weather not too severe I'm coming down in a motor with Miss Edy, just for two days. Then I may spend Holy week at the farm—not sure—I'll send orders about food later on—get the rooms warm and no smokey chimneys. Fancy 15 wee ducks! Delightful.' Further instructions followed, her secretary writing to the manager on 25th March to say 'The Mistress says she's coming down very soon now. Of course keep the pony harness and cart going daily nice and clean'; and then a further letter to his wife on 6th April to say 'Miss Terry says she will have had luncheon on Saturday before she arrives at the Farm, so have tea laid out very nicely—all one set of china (not mixed), nice snowy cloth and the best tray.'

Shaw met her daily during rehearsals and in his introduction to their published letters he says he speculated that with Irving dead and her heart vacant, there might be a chance of his filling the vacancy. He was married and does not enlarge on precisely what his intentions were. In any case, whatever he had in mind failed to materialise as Ellen's heart was not to be vacant for long.

While rehearsing *Brassbound* Ellen encountered a young American actor called James Carew who played Captain Kearney, the American naval officer. Ellen, according to Shaw, took one look at him and pocketed him. He was a ruggedly handsome man, similar in build to her second husband, Charles Kelly. Shaw wrote to Ellen four days before the opening of the play to say he was furiously jealous of Carew 'with whom you fell in love at first sight.'

Carew, born in Indiana in the 1870s, was of German-Jewish parentage, his real name being Usselman. He had wanted to act ever since seeing Ellen and Irving in Chicago, and he had made his first appearance in London the preceding year with Maxine Elliott in *Her Own Way*, then in 1906 was Hector Malone in Shaw's *Man and Superman*. In the 1930s—he died in 1938—he became one of the best-known actors in London, famous for his black-face cross-talk act, 'Alexander and Mose.'

But Ellen's interest in Carew was put on hold while London celebrated her stage jubilee in the June of 1906. There was a star matinee at Drury Lane, followed by a public banquet presided over by the Rt Hon Winston Churchill. A testimonial fund was also opened. When Ellen first saw the draft programme she was amazed to find that the programme was nearly entirely all-male. She could hardly speak for laughter at the idea of an actress-less programme in honour of an actress, so the (all-male) Executive Committee graciously added a series of tableaux in which the leading London actresses could appear.

The queues for the matinee—which included Ellen appearing in a scene from *Much Ado About Nothing* with all the available members of her family—started 24 hours beforehand. Ellen, visiting those camping out in front of the theatre at midnight, shook their hands and ordered coffee for them. There was a roll-call of honour of those also appearing on stage. Celebrities included Caruso singing; W S Gilbert presenting *Trial by Jury*; Mrs Patrick Campbell reciting; and the actress Eleonora Duse from Italy. There were music hall players (including Mr Seymour Hicks and all the Bath Buns) and one of Ted's masked dances—though he himself remained abroad. The whole show lasted five hours and brought in over £6,000 benefit to Ellen. She wrote to a friend, Austin Brereton, on 18th June to say 'I can't tell you how pleased I am to retire into semi-private life again and cease to worry my friends and the public.'[5]

When Ellen was in her King's Road house in London that year, James Carew was a frequent visitor. Ted received a letter from her, which he assumed referred to Carew, saying she had gone on the river 'with a very nice man—I am so sick of being eternally with crowds of women—they just bore me.' Carew's obvious admiration helped restore her confidence in herself as both woman and actress.

Ellen took a break after *Captain Brassbound's Conversion* to go down to Smallhythe and her letter to Shaw that November was a throwback to the old Harpenden days: 'I drive about wet or shine in an open "shay," eat fish and vegetables (heaps in the garden! Jolly! Do you like Salsify?), make curtains and do heaps of needlework jobs in the evenings, and the days fly by in a flash!'[6]

Ellen had agreed to go on a winter tour to America with *Captain Brassbound's Conversion* and two other plays under the management of Charles Frohman. She told him that she wanted James Carew as her leading man and he was cast as Captain Brassbound and also as Geert in *The Good Hope*.

Ellen and Carew impetuously married in Pittsburg in March 1907 amid great secrecy. Ellen wrote lyrically about Pittsburg to Shaw on 7th April saying 'Pittsburg, of all places in the world, is lovely! Surely, never was there more beautiful sunshine than today's!' At that point, she had been married to Carew a couple of weeks, but she said nothing about it. In her notes to Ellen's edited autobiography, Christopher St John writes that Ellen 'was in the toils of one of those strange infatuations which seem to us stranger when women

Ellen and Edy on board ship, along with the dog, in 1906. They were en route to America for another tour, with Edy as stage manager.

of strong character and great talent are their victims. A young American actor in the cast of *Brassbound* had the embarrassing privilege of putting Bernard Shaw's nose out of joint.'[7]

Edy and Chris had accompanied her on the tour, with Edy, unemployed, acting as her stage manager. Ellen praised her to Shaw ('She is so able, and such a Duck'), asking him, yet again, if he could offer her some work on the company's return.

Ellen ended her letter with 'James Carew goes on trying and striving and acts better and better every week. He is a splendid fellow and adores you, and me!'[8] She only told the company about her marriage when the tour was over and they were leaving for England. What was particularly strange was that she did not even tell Edy. Once the news was known, as they boarded the return ship home, Chris went to Ellen's cabin to reproach her for being so unfeeling to Edy in not confiding in her. According to Chris, this made Ellen regard her for some time as if she was infectious.

Ellen's reluctance to tell Edy may just have been to avoid recriminations: James Carew, after all, was only 34, younger than Edy, four years younger than Ted and 25 years younger than Ellen. Edy was to say, caustically, 'I give it two years.' Her son agreed the marriage would not last, saying of his mother: 'Her husbands were not to blame—it was she who was not a marriageable person—because she was too passionately the servant of the stage…I don't see how you can rock the cradle, rule the world, and play Ophelia perfectly, all in the day's work'.[9]

Carew, like Ellen's second husband Charles Kelly, was what Edy despised, a hunk of a man. But he was what Ellen wanted: a kind, thoughtful man, protective of Ellen and devoted to her. He remained so all his life. Even after her death he referred to her as 'My lady.' She was extremely happy in his company.

After their marriage, Ellen and Carew spent the summer on tour around the provinces in *Brassbound*. Shaw, now aware of the marriage, laughingly told her not to play Carew off the stage with her tricks, but she replied that 'James hasn't jilted me yet. He bosses me nicely instead.'

Nevertheless, he became sick of constantly playing in *Brassbound* and Ellen wrote to Shaw in October 1907 to say did he not think that she or her husband could play in his *Devil's Disciple*? She said they had to work and had no option other than wandering round the provinces, unless he could offer them something.

A follow-up letter had Ellen admitting that the part had now really got on her husband's nerves. 'He is not tied to my apron strings (nor is "his mother" tied to his) and if one of us is at work I shall be satisfied and so will he. I'd like you (for he loves you) to make him an offer. Oh, do be quick and ask him to play a fine part with a fair salary, or a mere good part with an unfair salary! Will you? Quick quick, oh, Shaw, and save us from the "Halls" or the Hells.' She ended rather wistfully saying they would both like to settle down at Smallhythe and do nice work.[10]

Ellen may have claimed she would like to settle down, but she still quite happily behaved like a teenager when the mood took her. Around this time she went to pay a formal 'bride call' on Mrs Hodgson Burnett, who lived near to her at Smallhythe in luxurious surroundings which included a lake, cedar trees, and

MR & MRS JAS. CAREW (MISS ELLEN TERRY)

Ellen at Smallhythe with her third husband, actor James Carew, whom she married in America in 1907 amid great secrecy. The marriage alienated Edy.

a paved terrace from which a steep slope of grass led to the lawn. Ellen took one look at it and decided it was a splendid place to roll down. She had a brown gown and brown cloak on at the time and when her hostess, greatly amused, rescued her at the bottom, she looked precisely like a long brown cigar.

Despite Ellen's pleas to Shaw ('Am I too old? I must act'), no work was forthcoming. Ellen, giving up the idea of work in England, booked a further tour of *Brassbound* to America for the autumn of 1908, telling Shaw that she hoped her husband would not be coming with her. 'I know I shall hate it without him, but it is dreadful for a man of his age to be playing one part year after year.' She told Shaw that they were both extraordinarily happy together and it was sad that they had to go different ways for a while, but that she knew James would go quite mad if faced with constantly playing the same part. 'He must do other work.'[11] Her hope that she and her husband would only be going different ways for a while remained just that, a hope.

Another factor was Edy. The marriage struck at the complicated, mutually possessive relationship she had with her mother. The jealous tensions aroused during the Martin Shaw affair promptly re-surfaced, only this time on Edy's side. Ted recalled his sister being 'utterly distraught' being 'prejudiced in some odd way against the male sex.' Both Ellen and Edy seemed unable to accept the other having a marital relationship, both seeing it as a threat to their own relationship. Edy loathed the idea of a married Ellen living in the farmhouse adjacent to the cottage that Ellen had given her at Smallhythe. She behaved as selfishly as Ellen had done over Martin Shaw, refusing to visit Ellen if Carew was there, and even locking the gate between the houses.

In June 1908 Ellen wrote rather miserably to her, saying, 'I hope it's not we are keeping you away from the cottage! That wd be too absurd —if you don't want to see us, there is space between the houses you know!' She added that she had fallen over and bruised herself black and blue, but that otherwise she was well and very happy 'except for one thing.' She underlined the word 'one' four times.[12]

Edy was impervious to her mother's pleas, even though Ellen wrote again to her saying, 'I don't go to the cottage because I can't go anywhere where Jim can't go—and is not welcomed— never mind.' All the services had been shared between the two houses, but Ellen realised 'of course now it wd never do. I am your most loving old mother.' She was very upset at this severance of relations, finally writing to Edy in a mixture of disapproval and underlying affection:

'I consider you are a very badly behaved young person but that

197

Ellen's husband, James Carew, was younger than her own son. The couple constantly toured in Captain Brassbound's Conversion, *but lack of other work put strains on the marriage and it only lasted some two years.*

I love you most dearly and trust you will see your way to leave off being a cruel and belligerent young woman as soon as you conveniently can, for it is a foolish behaviour which is commonly adopted by common girls and I can never class you with them in my mind.'[13]

Ellen was still worried about work, which caused her financial as well as personal stress. She was only too pleased to be offered a part in Graham Robertson's play for children, *Pinkie and the*

Fairies at Her Majesty's Theatre in the Christmas of 1908, writing to him to say, 'Blow the trumpets, beat the drums! I am delighted, my dear!' But she wrote to a friend in the summer of 1909 to say she couldn't afford certain items 'until Jim or I get some work—or sell a house, or sell each other or something.' To another she wrote, 'Did you say anything about James as "James Hook" (Capt Hook)? I'm sure he would be very good in the part.'[14] That autumn Carew at last managed to get a part in a touring company and Ellen joined him in Edinburgh.

The marriage, however, was fraying under these different strains and the two unofficially separated. Only then did Edy come back jubilantly down the path to her mother's house. From then on she acted as 'manager' to her mother.

Nevertheless, James Carew and Ellen remained warm friends all their lives: he continued to read scripts to her to save her eyesight, which was very poor, while Ellen was still to ask Shaw for work for him. They still spent time together, even building a workroom for James at the bottom of Ellen's tiny garden in Chelsea. Carew accidentally left his boots at Smallhythe when he finally left and Ellen always wore them. She still signed herself Ellen Carew and he still came to visit her, although when she was in her late seventies she sometimes failed to recognise him.

Her loneliness was offset by the affection of her new grandchildren, Nellie born in 1904 and Teddy in 1905. They were the children of Ted and Elena Meo. Ted had met Elena, daughter of the artist Gaetano Meo, in 1900 and she remained the love of his life. She accepted his sudden passions for other women, including Isadora Duncan with whom Ted had a child, Deirdre, later tragically drowned in the Seine. Ellen was, according to Chris St John, 'daft about Elena', their mutual interest being Ted to whom they were both totally devoted.

In an entry in a notebook around 1914, Ellen writes: 'For the last four years Elena and her two wonderful children, my most beloved grandchildren, have lived with me, and I am most happy, and not alone.'[15]

Ellen had carefully studied the characters of the Shakespearean women she played and when asked to lecture on them was able to refer to her copious notes. She considered Shakespeare had created heroines who were gallantly independent, high-spirited, intellectual, fearless and loveable. Her conclusions were neither facile nor 'actressy'.

Shakespeare *J* on stage

Ellen's interest in Shakespeare's heroines—she is seen here as Katherine of Aragon in Henry VIII— ed her to write and perform lectures on the subject.

Shakespeare on stage

Ellen was having to face up to the sad fact that despite having been the most lauded actress in England, her serious acting career was over. In the November of 1909 she appeared as Nance Oldfield in *A Pageant of Great Women* at the Scala Theatre. It was written by Cecily Hamilton and showed Woman, pleading with Justice for social and political liberty, with Prejudice, a man, arguing against her. A number of famous women supported the women's cause. Organised by Edy, Ellen called it 'the finest practical piece of political propaganda' and after a successful tour it led Edy into the field of political theatre.

In 1911 Edy founded the Pioneer Players which aimed to present plays that dealt with current social, political and moral ideas. Virginia Woolf called them 'the Pioneers of pain' as the subjects they tackled were indeed painful. As a theatre club it was not subject to censorship from the Lord Chancellor's Office so could, and did, stage Shaw's *Mrs Warren's Profession*, which was banned from public performance.

Ellen was the president, Edy the managing and stage director and Chris St John the secretary. Two of the members of the advisory committee were Bernard Shaw and Laurence Housman but the rest were women. Over the next few years Edy produced a series of crusading propaganda plays on subjects from suffrage to sex discrimination, which were highly successful in promoting the women's cause.[1] She and Chris were deeply involved with the suffrage movement, running a 'safe house'.

One of the plays staged was the drama *The Surprise of His Life* about a pregnant woman who refused to marry the father of her child. Ironically, the author was Jess Dorynne—the woman Ted had made pregnant after his marriage failed, then deserted. The press called it 'a brief for bastardy.'

That year, 1911, Ellen gave a lecture-recital on Shakespeare's heroines at the Kingsway Theatre in front of a Pioneer Players audience. The idea for doing this, an unexpected departure from acting, had originated the previous year when Ellen was depressed and baffled at having no work offered to her.

She was approached by the literary agents Curtis Brown, who asked her if she would do a lecture tour around America on Shakespeare's heroines. It would last from the November of 1910 to the spring of 1911. Ellen agreed and the tour proved immensely successful. She had lively and forceful views on the characters concerned after a lifetime spent in studying them and was passionate about Shakespeare.[2] Indeed her grandson Edward Craig said that Ellen talked about Shakespeare so much and in such a familiar way that he always believed Shakespeare was his grandfather. On stage, to reinforce her argument, Ellen acted excerpts from the plays. This revived the past for her and enchanted her audience.

The American venture was very successful and she was feted wherever she went. Lena Ashwell, a great friend of Ellen's who once worked at the Lyceum, came across her there. Courageous, undefeated, young at heart, Ellen hugged her friend and said, 'What do you think of me Lena? Sixty three, and on one-night stands'. Ellen was actually 64, but still continued to think she was a year younger.

In view of her success Ellen decided to try out the lectures in England and in the autumn of 1911 toured the provinces. Worried that the word 'lecture' sounded too academic and would frighten off audiences, the show was billed as 'A Shakespearean Discourse with Illustrative Acting.' It still did not sound like a fun night out, but nevertheless it drew in the crowds.

Always conscious of visual impression Ellen, helped by Edy, designed the stage setting carefully. She dressed in flowing robes of crimson, white or grey against a background of dark green

Ellen's Shakespearean lectures were highly popular. Touring America with them, she told a friend, 'What do you think of me? Sixty-three and on one-night stands'.

curtains, with bunches of flowers around the stage and ingenious lighting. Ellen had as a lectern one of the decorative desks she and Irving had used when they gave readings from *Macbeth* in 1889. Because her eyesight was so poor she had her lecture printed in extremely large bold type. As she could not resist scribbling extra comments all over it, she still found it hard to read. Fortunately she knew the different parts by heart.

Ellen's lectures, however, were far from a recitation of speeches by the various women in Shakespeare's plays. Particularly interesting was her opinion that the feminists of her day, whose views were considered highly radical, were no more radical than the feminists of the 15th and 16th centuries who were characters in Shakespeare's plays—like Beatrice in *Much Ado About Nothing*.

Ellen's conclusions were neither facile nor 'actressy': she gave her lectures a great deal of thought and they covered a number of issues. The following excerpt from one of them shows the reasoning behind her feminist interpretations:

'Shakspere [sic] created heroines who were gallantly independent high-spirited, intellectual, fearless, as well as loveable...Many people seem to think that the early Victorian woman is the type which has always been good enough for the world and would be good enough now, if a few violent spirits had not in recent days started a revolution.

'If you ask people with these views how they account for Shakspere's heroines, who certainly have more in common with our modern revolutionaries than with the fragile domestic ornaments of the thirties and forties, you will probably be told that Shakspere had to make his heroines like that, because the women's parts in plays were always played by young men!' This, Ellen admitted, explained why heroines were often dressed in boys' clothes, but said 'it had little to do with their characteristics. These have a much deeper significance.'

Although she knew many agreed that Shakespeare had liberal ideas about women, she thought they attributed this to his imagination. 'They don't seem to realise that the real women of his time were no fools.' Every generation, in her view, believed it was entirely different from the one preceding it. 'Such as prejudice exists even among the clever women of the present day, who appear quite

206

unconscious that the burning questions that they are discussing now are as old as the hills.' She thought this threw light on aspects that could otherwise be puzzling in Shakespeare's women.

Ellen pointed out that there had been a women's movement in the 15th century, when girls as well as boys were educated, women's opinions were deferred to and their position, though different, was important and dignified. 'We find that at first some people poked fun at this movement very much as to-day they poke fun at the Suffragettes.'

Regarding Queen Katharine of Aragon in *Henry VIII*, as 'one of Shakspere's noblest heroines', she said her Spanish tutor, Vives, had 'worked heart and soul for the higher education of Englishwomen: it was not so much emancipation that he preached as self-improvement.' She argued that whenever women have improved themselves they have attained freedom, rising to their responsibilities when called on to replace men in the council chamber and battlefield. Shakespeare, she thought, had been influenced by their freedom 'from priggishness and pedantry. Latin and Greek did not dry up their real and ardent emotions.' She considered that learning became a pose in the 18th century, bringing a reaction against learned women 'of which we have not yet seen the end.'

She spoke at length of the various 'heroines.' About Beatrice in *Much Ado About Nothing*, for example, she said the first thing she was sure of when studying the part was that 'the mind and the heart both rule.' Beatrice, she said, was brought up and educated by men and her uncles enjoy her talk, despite their reproofs. Leonardo may tell Beatrice that she will never get a husband 'if thou be so shrew of they tongue' but Ellen points out that he says it 'with a kind of affectionate pride and it is most important for an actress to see this.'

Ellen's lectures about the major female characters in Shakespeare that she had studied were lively and thought-provoking. *The Times* critic, who heard one of her lectures at the Haymarket Theatre in 1911, said that 'wherever and whenever Ellen Terry speaks, it will always be different and always fresh.'[3]

Nevertheless, although her lectures were highly successful they did not compensate Ellen for the lack of acting work. In any case

Ellen aboard ship in 1914, leaving for Australia. She wanted to do war work but her only offer was to lecture abroad on Shakespeare's Heroines.

she was so far from well, indeed near to breakdown, that in 1912 she went into a home for a 'rest cure.'

She still accepted a proposal that she embark on a world lecturing tour, starting in Melbourne, Australia, in May 1914. It was taking a gamble with her health—indeed a doctor told her that her heart was in such a condition she should not even walk upstairs and that any exertion might be fatal. Ellen called her heart 'a kicking donkey.' She admitted 'This discoursing is exhausting work, far more exhausting than playing a part, for I have to sustain the burden of the whole entertainment for nearly two hours. And then there is the travelling.'[4]

She was 67 at the start of this tour but needed the money to support her many dependents, currently an allowance for her daughter Edy on which Chris also lived; hand-outs on demand from Ted; the alimony for Ted's ex-wife May; paying for Godwin's son (by his second wife Beatrice) to go to Canada and supporting Charles Kelly's first wife's sisters.

On her way to Australia the boat had stopped at Naples and to her delight Ted, now living in Italy with Elena and their two children, came aboard and they went off together for a long drive. 'Red letter day', she wrote in her diary.

When she arrived in Australia the press were waiting. The Melbourne journal *The Age* lyrically described her as 'tall, graceful and fair-featured...the beauty that helped to make her what she is has not gone with her youth. It is a beauty of mind and expression as well as of feature.'[5] She was asked about her husband, James Carew, and told them 'He is often down [at Smallhythe]...but he always wants to alter the old place and make it new—just like an American, isn't it'; and surprised the reporters by admitting her age which made the *Sun* comment that she was 'certainly the most unwomanly woman' to have visited their country for some time.

Ellen further surprised the press by announcing 'you all know I'm a suffragette. Of course I am, and so is my daughter, Edith Craig.' This was a rare admission by Ellen. She had never appeared on a suffrage platform or gone on any marches supporting the suffragettes. She had reached the top of her own profession—she was the highest paid actress in England—without ever having encountered any discrimination and she was an example of a liberated woman.

209

Ellen's agreement to carry out a world lecture tour, beginning in Australia, was against her doctor's advice. Her heart by then was in a poor condition.

Katharine Cockin makes the point that 'it was Ellen Terry's unconventional life off stage as well as her fame and subsequent financial independence which had made her a "freewoman"... she defied every convention regarding women except with respect to the duties of a mother and the demands faced by a star from her

adoring public...' What is surprising is the way both public and authorities accepted her nonconformist behaviour.[6]

Ellen told the Australian press decisively that she thought women should have the vote, although dissociating herself from strong action like smashing windows. 'I'm an ardent suffragette, but I don't believe in all their militancy', she told *The Age*:

'It antagonises people and women never do any good that way. The suffragettes are a magnificent lot of women, but I think, perhaps, their ardour carries them away at times. And it shouldn't, it shouldn't. It makes them lose their poise and poise is everything.' This last sentence seems strikingly at odds with the philosophy of the *fin de siècle* 'new woman', but Cockin points out that Ellen 'never renounced femininity and was disturbed by the extreme challenge to femininity which suffrage militancy entailed.'[7]

Indeed, after a summer of hunger strikes four years previously, Ellen had written to a friend, Anna Methven, to say, 'Edy I believe comes to her cottage on Tuesday next—God knows I'll be glad to see her—although doubtless she will discourse now upon no subject but Womans Suffrage—Pardon the blot but 'Womans Suffrage" agitates me always and makes me sling the ink about.'[8] She wrote to Ted to say, 'Folk want me to vote—I won't—a dangerous thing to do without knowledge—I love loyalty to the King that is set up —believe, however, that in my heart I am a good democrat—but oh, I see this way and that way—and a wobbler like that does mischief. I'm not clever. I'm a fool—So knowing Fools are very dangerous in times like these, I shall leave it to old Edy and Co who will plump of course for Labour.'[9]

After her first lecture in Australia, Ellen wrote in her diary that she felt very ill and very nervous, 'but I let myself go! I dont think they liked it much, however.' The tour started successfully but Ellen then became seriously ill. Writing to her sister Kate from Melbourne on 15th August she told her she had had to give up the tour after only six performances to go into a private hospital for more than three weeks. 'You should see me! A very thin woman!! and my skin hanging on me like an Elephants! My illness and the scare and grief of this war to everyone has put an end to my lectures and to people going to theatres or to entertainments of any kind—my tour has been pretty well spoiled...'[10]

She wrote again to her sister to say she had visited Melba for a day and that she had 'a lovely home—great hills around and her garden is superb—she sang for me and was in splendid spirits.' Ellen went to stay with her for a month or so, though told her sister it was 'always England for me to abide in.'[11] She was to write anxiously to Edy about the Germans: 'Maybe they are in Kent by now, perhaps inhabiting our cottages! And perhaps you may be giving them some tea?' She added that the

On my 70th birthday =
27. Feb 1918 =

horrors of the war 'make me crazy, when I dare think, but I daren't, and only pray that no harm comes near you, and that somehow or another we meet at home before Christmas.'[12] She would write in her diary 'What madness! Thousands of lives lost today to gain ten yards in a little field.'

She did not see Edy again until the following May as she was advised to go home via America and continue her lecture tour there. Writing to Kate from New York in the November of 1914 she told her the lectures were 'proving a grand go and it relieves me to know that here in America at least I can come with a certainty of a welcome which will keep me flying! (It is of no use to me to crawl).' She admitted, however, that 'the strennosity [sic] of it all is not for the aged one.'[13]

An American reporter who interviewed her the following day noticed she was knitting. She explained that this was not for the war effort. 'It would have to be a terribly strong soldier who could wear anything that I knit for him.'

Ellen's eyesight had deteriorated even further in Australia and now, in America, her eyes were causing her so much pain that she decided to consult what she called an 'eyesmith.' He told her he must operate immediately on a cataract on her left eye and she told her sister she would have to be in hospital for three weeks. She wrote in her diary on 16th March 1915 'the tons of depression that have weighed on me, and anguished me, since the operation, are rolling away. New life and joy!'[14] She felt her own sufferings were cast in the shade by the news that Sarah Bernhardt had had a leg amputated. She cabled Paris '...You frightened me, but you are ever young and ever triumphant. Congratulations. Devotedly, E T.'

On Shakespeare's birthday, 23rd April 1915, Ellen gave what turned out to be her last performance in New York. She was 'nervous and weak at first. Soon inspired by the warmth of the audience' and she had to take off her long string of amber beads, apologising to the audience with the words 'The weight of them is too much for me.' Later a commemorative 'appreciation' was printed on handmade paper, saying how beautiful she looked in her red gown with its long flowing sleeves.

Ellen had a narrow escape on her return as she was offered a comfortable suite on the *Lusitania* on 1st May, which was torpedoed, and only refused it because she had promised Edy not to travel on an English boat. She was deeply grieved by the tragic death of Irving's son Laurence when the *Empress of Ireland* went down.

On her return, to her astonishment and indignation, she was asked to register as an alien—as she had married the American

Ellen was quite happy to act in an amateur Nativity Play at Rye, near to her Smallhythe house. It was produced by her daughter Edy.

James Carew. She blankly refused, saying what nonsense, she was English and always had been, and the matter was dropped.

The war had ended Ellen's hopes of making money from her lecture tour and she wrote to Kate from her Chelsea house in August to ask if she knew of anyone 'in these bad days' who would like to buy the farmhouse at Smallhythe. She told her she regretted leaving 'chubby Bertha', her maid, in New York despite the fact that 'her tidiness made her just shove things out of sight and swear I wanted new ones.' She added that 'to travel even a little distance now appals me.'[15]

That year J M Barrie's play *The Admirable Crichton* was revived with a star cast for a matinee in aid of a war charity. Barrie especially wrote in for Ellen the part of an old housekeeper. She also appeared in a ballet—pantomime called *The Princess and the Pea* at the Haymarket, in aid of 'The Invalid Kitchens of London' in which her two grandchildren, Nellie and Teddy, also had walk–on parts.

215

Ellen's life went on uneventfully, as seen through her letters to her sister Kate ('Kitty').[16] Writing to her from Chelsea on 30th December 1915 she said she was just back from Wales with a small company which had been going around to small towns 'with a few curtains and dresses' and giving 'quite a good little entertainment.' This consisted of recitals by Ellen, with some one-act plays by the other members. They never made less than £30 a performance.

She told Kate that Marion, their sister, had joined her at Christmas in Chelsea 'to partake of goose and Xmas pudding, followed by pills and Stolitz Powders.' Ellen said she was looking forward to getting down to Smallhythe (fortunately still unsold), and would be putting on a Nativity Play at nearby Rye.

During the following Christmas of 1916 she wrote to Kate from Smallhythe to tell her she was down with a high temperature, an overwhelming cold, and that 'the fatigue upon me just now is indescribable.' She couldn't, she wrote, even get to the local concert to recite *Daffodils*. Ted always claimed her illnesses were imaginary, but her letters constantly referred to her health. Writing again to Kate she said 'my eyes daze me and I'm pretty nervous from one cause and another' and from Llandrindod Wells she told her 'I am here for "a cure" for my neuritis in arm and foot.'

In 1916 Ellen, still on the lookout for means of making money, was pleased to be asked by the British Ideal Film Company to star in a film called *Her Greatest Performance*—although this title proved ironic as her screen performance hardly lived up to her stage acting. Ellen played the part of a retired actress whose son is wrongly accused of murder but who discovers her dresser (played by Edy) knows the real murderer. The dresser makes a death-bed confession and Ellen impersonates her, tricking the real murderer into admission of the crime. The film was released in 1917 to a tepid reception: the terrible real-life drama of the war absorbed everyone's attention.

Ellen sent Kate some signed photographs of her filming, saying she could not manage this before: 'I was too deadbeat to do anything but go to bed and sleep like a hog—exhausted.' She told her sister that 'Edy plays a Dresser and is very good in some of the scenes…I am even dirtier and horrid-er than she is—the Cinema life is a very trying life, exhausting in such weather as this and yet it is both amusing and profitable.'

A further film in 1918, *The Invasion of Britain*, sponsored by the Ministry of Information was never shown as the director failed to complete it before the end of the war. In all, Ellen made three more films: *The Pillars of Society*, *Potter's Clay* and *The Bohemian Girl*. According to Chris St John, Ellen 'showed in flashes that she was quite capable of adapting her flexible and fluid talent to a new medium, if she had been more intelligently directed.'[17]

Ellen herself never felt that the cinema was a good medium for actors, but when she was taken to see Valentino in *Blood and Sand*, she thought any young man about to play *Hamlet* should see it: 'That's the way to stand under the balcony.'

Throughout the war, Ellen appeared intermittently at shows to boost war charities in excerpts like the trial scene in *The Merchant of Venice*, though increasingly nervous of forgetting her words. While acting this particular scene at the Coliseum in 1918 there was an air raid and many younger artists were too panic-striken to reappear on stage. The manager told them they should be ashamed of themselves and to look at Ellen. 'She's an old woman and she's as cool as a cucumber. If she don't mind the bombs, why on earth should you?'

Edy meanwhile was constantly busy with productions for the Pioneer Players. The actress Margaret Webster remembered her sitting by a gasfire in a highly coloured dressing gown, 'just talking—telling stories, discussing, recalling, planning, prophesying, throwing out splinters of ideas with every sentence, sparks flying from her words…making herself a channel for the age-old "life-force" of the theatre.'[18]

Edy had none of Ellen's legendary charm and her brusque, direct manner often offended people. A born director, her undoubted ability won the respect of such actresses as Sibyl Thorndike. Nevertheless, she was unable to get work. Even her success in running the entire season's productions at the Everyman Theatre, Hampstead in 1921 led nowhere. Ellen, asking Lilian Baylis, the manager of the Old Vic Theatre, if she could offer Edy work, received the reply: 'We don't want another woman here. And

In 1919 Ellen played the part of the Nurse in Romeo and Juliet. *John Gielgud, who saw her, said she could still enchant audiences.*

anyhow we don't want Edy. She would upset the staff.'[19] *The Times* made the valid point, in Edy's obituary, that 'her devotion to her mother shone out more brightly than the remarkable theatrical talent which never, perhaps, received its due attention.'

However, Edy was happy enough. She and Chris had become friendly with Radclyffe Hall, the author of *Well of Loneliness*, and Una Troubridge, who lived together in Rye, and they all light-heartedly drove round Kent in a pony cart. Edy had also asked Clare Atwood (Tony) to share Priest's House at Smallhythe with her and Chris. The ménage a trois that resulted (Vita Sackville-West called them 'The Trouts') was very successful as Tony, an artist, was a pleasant, quiet woman who kept the peace.

Ellen, back in Chelsea in the summer of 1918, asked her sister to find her a 'nice steady quiet young Home Parlourmaid.' She laid down the rules: 'Every third Sunday she can go out and once a week in the evening for a few hours—I treat them to a theatre once a month and I raise their wages after the second year, £1. I expect them downstairs before seven and they can be in bed by ten every evening for we seldom dine late or have hot suppers.' She ends by asking Kitty to visit her. 'Let's be devils!! And go, first, to a restaurant and dinner (shortly) and after to The Palace or some other Music Hall!!!'[20]

This implies that Ellen was reasonably fit, but she wrote to Lillian Baylis that November to explain why she had missed that season's performances at the Old Vic: 'I enclose you a small picture of myself, so you may note I am not as young as I was and I could not risk the possibility of being obliged to walk to and from the theatre. Cabs were scarce—omnibuses too hasty for me and I have not as yet achieved wings.' She congratulated Lillian Baylis and her company for having carried on, despite wartime problems.[21] Despite Ellen's failing sight, many of her letters asked theatre managers for a box, where she sat holding up her mother-of-pearl inlaid opera glasses, gold-stamped with her initials.

Ellen's last appearance in a full-length Shakespeare production was in 1919 as the Nurse in *Romeo and Juliet*. She wrote to Margaret Steen to say, 'I'm keeping all the rude bits in.'

Ellen remained spirited, even in her last years. She made
an occasional brief stage appearance (with the words
pinned to the stage furniture) and wrote in her diary that
she was unhinged, though not unhappy. In 1925, at the
age of 78, Ellen was finally made a Dame

A

'Ariel in the tree'

Christmas, 1920. With difficulty Ellen reads the dialogue of a Nativity Play at the Everyman Theatre. Clemence Dane described her as 'Ariel in the Tree'.

'Ariel in the tree'

Ellen had long been living beyond her means. By 1921 she was virtually bankrupt due to her obstinately subsidising myriad dependents, giving to charities and maintaining two houses. She went down to stay with Graham Robertson, who told a friend she was leaving her 'dear little Chelsea house' where he found she had been staying all alone without a fire. She relinquished control of her money to trustees, who included the editor of *The Morning Post*, the husband of a friend. They stopped her outflow of money. Used to handling her own affairs, and earning sufficient money to cover her outgoings, she was bewildered by her changed circumstances.

Ellen moved to a tiny flat in St Martin's Lane which Ted, in London a year later to open his International Exhibition of Theatre Art and Craft at the Victoria and Albert Museum, scornfully described as 'most un-Terrylike.' She did not really need a house as on medical advice, she was leading a very quiet life. But it was not all downhill: although constantly stumbling because of her dimmed eyesight, she still managed to visit her favourite restaurant, the Gourmet in Lisle Street, and was within walking distance of at least five theatres. Edy was nearby in a Bedford Street flat and James Carew lived practically next door. Servants found Ellen difficult, however, and she was blacklisted on agency lists. She luckily took on a Yorkshire woman, Hilda Barnes (Barney), who became devoted to her, jealously guarded her and acted as servant, protector and friend during her last years.

223

Ellen was increasingly dependent now on Edy, even if sometimes resenting this situation. As Nina Auerbach, a biographer of Ellen Terry says: 'Now here was her daughter, reflecting and restraining her like the others' even if Ellen 'could not, from the beginning, let Edy go'.[1]

Ellen wrote in her diary on 26th April 1921: 'I am unhinged (not unhappy) and uncomfortable. I wonder where everything is. Cannot remember new things. All is changed. Change at 73 puzzles the will. I live in puzzledom.'[2] Yet her white hair still grew luxuriantly, her figure remained slender and supple, and her voice still had tone and volume. Despite cutbacks, she remained in a panic about money and that July signed up for a week's engagement, for £100, at the Gaiety Theatre in Manchester. 'Edy needs a hundred pounds', she said.[3]

The following February Edy went to Egypt for six weeks and Ellen wrote dejectedly to Marguerite Steen to say 'I do nothing from day to day, and it is an AWFUL waste of time—and of course I am bored—think of that!! My memory frayed to smithereens and 'there is no health in me.' I feel rather like hating everything—a bad state of things—CIRCULATION IS LACKING—I FEEL SURE THAT IS THE TROUBLE.'[4]

She cheered up, however, after participating in a few more charity matinees and when she unveiled a memorial tablet to Sarah Siddons at Bath, Marguerite Steen recalled her driving in an open carriage through the city accompanied by her old friend Squire Bancroft. They pretended to be minstrels, singing a music hall song with Ellen shaking a non-existent tambourine.

Throughout the early 1920s Ellen received many affectionate letters from her grandchildren, Nelly and Teddy, then living in Villa Raggio, Rapallo, Italy. 'Dear Granny, I love you very much. How are you? Love from Teddy' came on a small pink card covered with kisses. Illustrations included 'papa playing the piano and mama siging' [sic], while Nelly wrote 'Dear Pet Granny. We miss you very much. I love you very much Granny Pet. I send kisses to you. From Nelly.'[5]

In 1922, Ellen received the honorary degree of LL.D from St Andrews University, telling Bernard Shaw that the Rector, J M Barrie, 'was almost as beautiful and adorable as my five months old

Despite Ellen complaining that her memory, in old age, was frayed to smithereens, her figure stayed supple and her voice kept its tone and volume.

225

Ellen unveils the memorial plaque to Mrs Siddons at the Siddons house in Bath. Alongside Ellen: the Mayor of Bath, Frederic Harrison, Sir Squire Bancroft.

kitten.' Barrie had bestowed the award because the tragedienne Genevieve Ward had just been made a Dame amid a growing awareness that Ellen was long overdue for public recognition. Only in 1925, at the age of 78, was Ellen made Dame Grand Cross of the Most Excellent Order of the British Empire. She was now so frail she was invested in a private room at Buckingham Palace, where she rose from her wheelchair to give a magnificent curtesy to the King. She and Queen Mary then reminisced about the old

days at the Lyceum. 'A lovely time', wrote Ellen in her diary.

Her final appearance on stage was also in 1925, in Walter de la Mare's *Crossings* at the Lyric Theatre in Hammersmith. Chris St John remembers her gliding across the stage, 'the spirit of beauty, rather than beauty itself [she] filled the spectators with a strange awe. A long sighing "Oh!" arose from them all, and the sound was a more wonderful tribute than any applause I have ever heard.'[5]

Ellen remembered her part less romantically as when she had asked the producer for instructions over her part he replied, 'Well you see–you–er–well, you come on.' Ellen waited. 'Well, then you–er–well–you come off again.'

Ellen spent most of next summer and autumn down at

Smallhythe but she then contracted bronchial pneumonia so seriously that Ted was sent for from Italy. This immediately cheered her up and convinced him she was not really ill at all. He returned to Italy and Ellen slowly recovered. Set on spending Christmas in London with Edy, four ambulancemen had to carry her up the stairs.

Graham Robertson, with whom Ellen frequently stayed, visited her early the next year in London and found her quite happy with Edy dropping in from time to time and her grandson Teddy staying. Only a month later, however, he wrote that Ellen was now 'very sadly' and was 'drifting away into a strange vague world where nothing is real and people bear no names.'[6] 'Ariel in the Tree' was the impression of Clemence Dane, the novelist.

Ellen did, however, recognise James Carew when he visited her on 7th March, saying 'Tell me, Jim, I can't quite remember—did I kick you out or did you kick me out?' Jim replied cautiously, 'Well dear, I think we arranged it between us, didn't we?' 'Yes, so we did,' said Nell. Then after a pause: 'Dam' fools, weren't we?'[7]

Because the heating was being repaired at Smallhythe, which was taking a considerable time, Ellen went on staying with friends, looked after by Barney rather to Edy's jealousy. Barney allayed this by writing constantly to Edy, giving news of Ellen. She told Edy her mother 'was still remarkably strong and was talking of joining her sister Marion in Monte Carlo, threatening she will take good care no one stops her going.'[8] Another letter said that Ellen had been 'terribly naughty the whole night wanting to wander out and look for me. I tried to stay in bed and let Miss Hassal cope with it, but once I had to go: a terrific noise was going on and things seemed to be flying round the room.'[9]

Ellen finally returned to Smallhythe in March 1928. She told the doctor, as she arrived in a wheelchair, 'This is my own house, bought with my own money.' She cheered up once at home, but said 'I hate being old. Yes, I just hate it. People are very kind, but that makes it worse. However, it's absurd to cry over spilt milk. I intend to go into my grave smiling.'[10]

The month of July was hot and on the 16th Ellen persuaded Barney and the nurse to wheel her outside. They left her parked in the road while they rested nearby and Ellen drew their attention by the simple means of throwing her shoe at them.

Ellen loved it when her grand-daughter Nellie came from her home in Italy, this time with her mother Elena Meo (centre).

Ellen at Smallhythe with her granddaughter Nellie Craig, of whom she was extremely fond. Nellie and her brother were Ted's children by Elena Meo.

Edy had left for London that day, but the next morning Barney rushed into Chris and Tony next door to tell them Ellen had had a stroke. Edy was immediately summoned back along with Ted who, by chance, was in London but had not yet visited Smallhythe, not

believing Ellen was that ill. Edy, on arrival, put on her smock so that her mother would see something familiar when she rallied.

But Ellen, paralysed by the stroke, did not rally and never opened her eyes again. The word spread that she was dying and her brothers Fred and Charlie, her sister Marion and niece Olive came down. Hundreds sent messages, including the King and Queen.

Edy sat constantly with her, holding her hand. Once, indistinctly,

Ellen in the rose garden she created at her Smallhythe house. She spent much time there saying, it brought her great peace of mind.

Ellen said the word 'Happy.' At 8.30 am on the morning of 21ˢᵗ July 1928, she died. In a copy of *The Imitation of Christ* which Barney found in her bedroom, Ellen had copied out on the flyleaf a poem by William Allingham:

No funeral gloom, my dears, when I am gone;
Corpse-gazings, tears, black raiment, graveyard grimness,

Think of me as withdrawn into the dimness,
Yours still, you mine. Remember all the best
Of our past moments, and forget the rest.
And so, to where I wait, come gently on.

Ellen had written under this the words, 'I should wish my children, relatives and friends to observe this when I die.' And indeed they did. The funeral was held on 24th July and a copy of the poem was pinned to the gate of Ellen's house. Edy in a pale suit, arm-in-arm with Ted who was holding a bunch of multi-coloured flowers, led the long, winding funeral procession of friends and relatives. The church was filled with the scent of country herbs, brought from Ellen's garden and strewn along the aisles. The only funeral gloom was shown by Mrs Aria, Irving's constant companion of his last years. She sobbed that by dying now, Ellen would get to Irving first.

The coffin, designed by Ted and covered in a gold pall, was taken to Golders Green crematorium. The ashes were then taken in a silver casket to St Paul's Church, Covent Garden, the actors' church. In the year it took to negotiate their permanent place there, a special room in Edy's flat was converted into an oratory, blessed, and the ashes were placed there under a constantly-burning sanctuary light. James Carew sent flowers there weekly. In his will, he asked that his own ashes be sprinkled at Smallhythe. His solicitor took the parcel of ashes down there but, according to Sir Donald Sinden, the door was opened by Chris, who told the solicitor 'We don't want that man here' and slammed the door. The parcel was then discovered the next day lying neatly on the grass and Chris and Edy promptly threw it in the nettlebed.

Edy sent Miss Bocking ('Bo'), a long-time member of the household and niece of Mrs Rumball ('Boo'), Ellen's first and much-loved housekeeper, some of her mother's things which she said she couldn't bear anyone 'except ourselves' to have. She told her that Ellen's death 'was so lovely and she was so happy and peaceful that you can't feel mournful or depressed. She would of so hated it. I'm making her two rooms at the Farm into a memorial but I have very little money and couldn't keep it up by myself so I

233

Ted and Edy head Ellen's Smallhythe funeral procession in 1928.

may sell it (as a memorial) and preserve it for ever.'[10] The farm, just as Ellen left it, is now preserved by the National Trust.

After Ellen's death, Edy lived on with Chris and Tony at their cottage in Smallhythe until her death in 1947—exactly a century since Ellen's own birth in 1847.

In that century there had been radical changes in the theatre: in the type of plays, their staging, the acting and audiences' attitudes. But Ellen—magnetic, vital, surpremely talented—stands out. She had a dancing gaiety that dazzled not only audiences but all those

she met. During a revival of *Much Ado About Nothing* in 1891 she wrote in her diary on 5th January:

'I must make Beatrice more flashing at first, and softer afterwards...She must be always merry and by turns scornful, tormenting, vexed, self-communing, absent, melting, teasing, brilliant, indignant, sad-merry, thoughtful, withering, gentle, humorous, and gay, Gay, Gay! Protecting (to Hero), motherly, very intellectual—a gallant creature and complete in mind and feature.'[11]

This, too, was Ellen.

Footnotes

Theatre in the blood

[1] Ellen Terry, *Ellen Terry's Memoirs* with preface, notes and additional biographical chapters by Edith Craig and Christopher St John (Victor Gollancz, London: 1933)
p10, hereinafter *ET/Memoirs*
[2] T. Edgar Pemberton, *Ellen Terry and Her Sisters (Arthur Pearson, London: 1902*),
p20, hereinafter Pemberton/*Terry*
[3] ET/*Memoirs*, p8
[4] ET/*Memoirs*, p44
[5] Pemberton/*Terry*, p24
[6] ET/*Memoirs*, p11
[7] ET/*Memoirs* p23
[8] ET/*Memoirs* p22
[9] Pemberton/*Terry*, p36
[10] ET/*Memoirs*, p32
[11] Pemberton/*Terry* p62
[12] ET/*Memoirs*, p35
[13] ET/*Memoirs*, p38
[14] Charles Hiatt, *Ellen Terry and Her Impersonations* (George Bell, London: 1899) p47
[15] Pemberton/*Terry*, p76

Wonderland goes sour

[1] ET/*Memoirs*, p43
[2] Ellen Terry and Bernard Shaw, *Ellen Terry and Bernard Shaw: A Correspondence*, ed Christopher St John (Constable, London: 1931) p111, hereafter ET/*Correspondence*
[3] Wilfrid Blunt, *England's Michelangelo* (Hamish Hamilton, London: 1975) p107
[4] The Watts Gallery archives
[5] Graham Robertson, *Letters of Graham Robertson*, ed Kerrison Preston (Hamish Hamilton, London: 1953) p111
[6] David Loshak, 'G.F. Watts and Ellen Terry' in *Burlington Magazine*,

November 1963

[7] *Punch* archives

[8] Watts Gallery archives

[9] Hebe Elsna, *The Sweet Lost Years* (Robert Hale, London: 1955) p57

[10] Marguerite Steen, *A Pride of Terrys* (Longmans, London: 1962) p96, hereinafter Steen/*Pride*

[11] Wilfrid Blunt, 'Watts and Ellen Terry,' in *Burlington Magazine*, January 1964

[12] ET/*Memoirs*, p45

[13] Ellen Terry, *The Story of My Life* (The Boydell Press, London: 1982) p33

[14] A.M.W. Stirling, *Life's Little Day* (Butterworth, London: 1924), p219

[15] A.M.W. Stirling, *Life's Little Day* (Butterworth, London, 1924) p220

[16] ET/*Memoirs*, p46

[17] Morton N. Cohen, *Lewis Carroll* (Macmillan, London: 1995) p237

[18] David Loshak, 'G.F. Watts and Ellen Terry' in *Burlington Magazine*, November 1963

[19] Watts Gallery archives

[20] The Theatre Museum archives, hereinafter TM

[21] TM

[22] ET/*Memoirs*, p46

[23] Ellen Terry Memorial Museum archives, hereinafter ETMM

[24] ETMM

[25] Lady Duff Gordon, *Discretions and Indiscretions* (Jarrolds, London: 1932) p33

[26] ET/*Memoirs*, p63

[27] ET/*Memoirs*, p48

[28] ET/*Memoirs*, p61

The world well lost for love

[1] Tom Prideaux, *Love or Nothing: The Life and Times of Ellen Terry* (Millington, London: 1976) p73

[2] ET/*Memoirs*, p66

[3] Laurence Irving, *Henry Irving: The Actor and His World* (Faber and Faber, London: 1951) p147, hereinafter Irving/*Irving*

[4] Graham Robertson, *Letters of Graham Robertson* ed Kerrison Preston (Hamish Hamilton, London: 1953) pp139-140

[5] ET/*Memoirs*, p68

[6] Edward Craig, *Gordon Craig: The Story of His Life* (Victor Gollancz, London: 1968) p39, hereinafter Craig/*Gordon Craig*

[7] Steen, *Pride*, p123

[8] W. Graham Robertson, *Time Was* (Hamish Hamilton, London: 1931) p140

[9] W. Graham Robertson, *Time Was* (Hamish Hamilton, London: 1931) p141

[10] Ellen Terry and Bernard Shaw, *Ellen Terry and Bernard Shaw: A Correspondence,* ed Christopher St John (Reinhardt & Evans, London: 1949) p87

[11] ETMM

[12] Craig/*Gordon Craig,* p95

[13] Edward Gordon Craig, *Index to the Story of My Days* (Hulton Press, London: 1957) p11, hereinafter Craig/*Index*

[14] Steen, *Pride*, p134

[15] ET/*Memoirs*, p192

[16] ET/*Memoirs*, p69

'Ellen Terry is an enigma'

[1] ET/*Memoirs*, p78

[2] Charles L. Reade and The Rev. Compton Reade, *Charles Reade* (Chapman and Hall, London: 1887) pp293-4

[3] Malcolm Elwin, *Charles Reade* (Jonathan Cape, London: 1931) p262

[4] Sir Johnston Forbes---Robertson, *A Player Under Three Reigns* (T. Fisher Unwin, London: 1925) pp66-67

[5] ET/*Memoirs*, p73

[6] ET/*Memoirs*, p83

[7] ET/*Memoirs*, pp70-71

[8] ETMM

[9] ET/*Memoirs*, p86

[10] J. Comyns Carr, *Mrs. J. Comyns Carr's Reminiscences*, ed Eve Adam (Hutchinson, London: 1928, p31

[11] W. Graham Robertson, *Time Was* (Hamish Hamilton, London:1931), p96

[12] ET/*Memoirs*, p88

[13] ET/*Memoirs*, p90

[14] Sir S. Bancroft and Lady Bancroft, *The Bancrofts: Recollections of Sixty Years* (John Murray, London: 1909) p203

[15] ETMM

[16] Craig/*Gordon Craig*, p46

[17] ET/*Memoirs*, p97

[18] Craig, *Gordon Craig: The Story of His Life*, p48

[19] Edward Gordon Craig, *Ellen Terry and Her Secret Self* (Sampson Low, Marston, London: 1931) p59

[20] ET/*Memoirs*, p109

[21] ET/*Memoirs*, p108

[22] Craig/*Index*, p25

[23] ET/ *Memoirs*, p116

[24] ET/*Memoirs* p113

Ellen & Irving: 'My own dear wife'

[1] Irving/*Irving*, p200

[2] Irving/*Irving*, p316

[3] ET/*Memoirs*, p130

[4] ET/*Memoirs*, p119

[5] ET/*Memoirs*, p121

[6] Irving/*Irving*, p372

[7] ET/*Memoirs*, p122

[8] ET/*Memoirs*, p122

[9] Charles Hiatt, *Ellen Terry* (George Bell, London: 1899) pp114-5

[10] ET/*Memoirs*, p128

[11] Sir Frank Benson, *My Memoirs* (Ernest Benn, London: 1930) p186

[12] ET/*Memoirs*, p125

[13] Craig/*Index*, p36

[14] Irving/*Irving*, p316

[15] ET/*Memoirs*, p120

[16] ET/*Memoirs*, p150

[17] Charles Hiatt, *Ellen Terry* (George Bell, London: 1899) p130

[18] ET/*Memoirs*, p115

[19] ET/*Memoirs*, p128

[20] Charles Hiatt, *Ellen Terry* (George Bell, London: 1899) p142

[21] Henry James, *The Scenic Art*, ed Allan Wade (Hill and Wang, New York: 1957) p143

[22] W. Graham Robertson, *Time Was* (Hamish Hamilton, London: 1931), p55-56

[23] ET/*Memoirs*, p117

[24] ET/*Correspondence*, p125

[25] Craig/*Index*, p49

[26] ET/*Memoirs*, p149

[27] ET/*Memoirs*, p269

[28] ETMM

[29] Tom Prideaux, *Love or Nothing: The Life and Times of Ellen Terry* (Millington, London: 1975) p136

[30] Roger Manvell, *Ellen Terry* (William Heinemann, London: 1968) p245

[31] Margaret Webster, *The Same Only Different* (Victor Gollancz, London: 1969) p191

[32] Steen/*Pride*, p185

[33] Nina Auerbach, *Ellen Terry: Player in Her Time* (J.M. Dent, London: 1987)p205

[34] Irving/*Irving*, p480

[35] Irving/*Irving*, p480

[36] Craig/*Index*, p48

[37] Irving/*Irving*, p366

[38] ET/*Memoirs*, p128

[39] Mrs Clement Scott, *Old Days in Bohemian London* (Frederick A. Stokes, New York: 1919) p117

[40] ET/*Memoirs*, p128

[41] *Letters of Graham Robertson*, ed Kerrison Preston (Hamish Hamilton, London: 1953) p261

[42] Steen/*Pride*, p190

[43] ET/*Memoirs*, p163

[44] Charles Hiatt, *Ellen Terry* (William Bell: London, 1899) p166

[45] ET/*Memoirs*, p167

[46] Craig/*Index*, p48

[47] Craig/*Index*, p56

[48] ET/*Memoirs*, p195

Conquering America

[1] Irving/*Irving*, p373

[2] ET/*Memoirs*, p208

[3] ET/*Memoirs*, p197

[4] ET/*Memoirs*, p207

[5] Irving/*Irving*, p430

[6] Craig, *Index*, p58

[7] Charles Hiatt, *Ellen Terry* (Ernest Benn, London: 1930) p177

[8] ET/*Memoirs*, p149

[9] Alice Comyns Carr, *Mrs J Comyns Carr's Reminiscences* (Hutchinson: London, 1928) p111, 113

[10] Blanche Patch, *Thirty Years with GBS* (Victor Gollancz, London: 1931) p104

[11] Irving/*Irving,* p444

[12] Irving/*Irving,* p448

[13] ETMM

[14] ET/*Memoirs,* p181

[15] Craig/*Gordon Craig,* p60

[16] ETMM

[17] ET/*Memoirs,* p97

[18] ETMM

[19] Alice Comyns Carr, *Mrs J Comyns Carr's Reminiscences* (Hutchinson: London, 1928) p155

[20] Craig/*Index,* p67

[21] ET/*Memoirs,* p187

[22] Lady Duff Gordon, *Discretions and Indiscretions* (Jarrolds: London, 1932) p33

[23] ET/*Memoirs,* p195

Lady Macbeth - no monster

[1] Craig/*Index,* pp110-111

[2] ET/*Memoirs,* p232

[3] ETMM

[4] ET/*Memoirs,* p233

[5] Irving/*Irving,* p504

[6] ETMM

[7] ET/*Memoirs,* p234

[8] ET/*Memoirs,* p235

[9] Craig/*Gordon Craig,* p73

[10] Craig/*Index,* pp125-26

[11] Craig/*Index,* p128

[12] ETMM

[13] ETMM

[14] ETMM

Ellen, Ellenor, Ellenest

[1] Irving/*Irving,* p570

[2] ET/*Memoirs,* p270

[3] Margaret Webster, *The Same Only Different* (Victor Gollancz, London: 1969), pp170-1) hereinafter Webster/*The Same*

[4] Webster/*The Same*, p175

[5] Webster/*The Same*, p176

[6] ET&BS/*Letters*, p60

[7] ET&BS/*Letters*, p97

[8] ET&BS/*Letters*, p105

[9] ET&BS/*Letters*, p229

[10] ET/*Memoirs*, p351

[11] Steen/*Pride*, p226

[12] ETMM

[13] ET/*Correspondence*, p245

[14] ET/*Memoirs*, p271

[15] ET/*Memoirs*, p272

[16] ET/*Correspondence*, p297

Edy: love takes all

[1] Christopher St John, *Edy*, ed Eleanor Adlard (Frederick Muller, London: 1949) p20

[2] Irene Cooper Willis, *Edy*, ed Eleanor Adlard (Frederick Muller, London: 1949) p107

[3] ET/*Correspondence*, p340

[4] ET/*Memoirs*, p274

[5] Irving/*Irving*, p633

[6] Christopher St John, *Hungerheart: The Story of a Soul* (Methuen, London: 1915), p224

[7] ETMM

[8] ET/*Correspondence*, p354

[9] TM

[10] TM

[11] ET/*Correspondence*, p367

[12] Craig/*Index*, p244

[13] ET/*Memoirs*, p256

[14] Edward Gordon Craig, *Ellen Terry and Her Secret Self* (Sampson Low, Marston, London: 1931) p139

[15] Edward Gordon Craig, *Ellen Terry and Her Secret Self* (Sampson Low, Marston, London: 1931) p135

[16] Craig/*Index*, p248

[17] Edward Gordon Craig collection, Biblioteque Nationale

[18] Christopher St John, *Hungerheart: The Story of a Soul* (Methuen, London: 1915), p235

[19] Christopher St John, *Hungerheart: The Story of a Soul* (Methuen, London: 1915), p227

[20] Edward Gordon Craig collection, BN

[21] Christopher St John, *Edy*, ed Eleonor Adlard (Frederick Muller, London: 1949) p22

[22] Steen/*Pride*, p210

[23] Irving/*Irving*, p652

The third marriage

[1] ET/*Memoirs*, p261

[2] ET/*Correspondence*, p373

[3] Irving/*Irving*, p671

[4] ETMM

[5] TM

[6] ET/*Correspondence*, p396

[7] ET/*Memoirs*, p266

[8] ET/*Correspondence*, p397

[9] Edward Gordon Craig, *Ellen Terry and Her Secret Self* (Sampson, Low, Marston: London, 1931) p47

[10] ET/*Correspondence*, p401

[11] ET/*Correspondence*, p403

[12] ETMM

[13] ETMM

[14] ETMM

[15] ET/*Memoirs*, p297

Shakespeare on stage

[1] Pioneer Players Reports, ETMM

[2] Ellen Terry, *Four Lectures on Shakespeare*, ed Christopher St John (Martin Hopkinson, London: 1932) and ETMM

[3] ET/*Memoirs*, p288

[4] ET/M*emoirs*, p288

[5] ET/*Memoirs*, p290

[6] Katharine Cockin, 'Slinging the Ink About: Ellen Terry and Women's Suffrage Agitation' in (ed) Caroline Bland and Maire Cross, Gender and Politics in the Age of Letter-Writing, 1750-2000 (Ashgate Publishing, Hampshire: 2004) pp203-4 hereinafter Cockin/*Ink*

[7] Cockin/*Ink*, p209

[8] ETMM

[9] Edward Gordon Craig, *Ellen Terry and Her Secret Self* (Sampson, Low & Marston, London: 1931) p134

[10] TM

[11] TM

[12] ET/*Memoirs*, p291

[13] TM

[14] ET/*Memoirs*, p294

[15] TM

[16] ETMM

[17] ET/*Memoirs*, p299

[18] Margaret Webster, *Edy*, ed Eleonor Adlard (Frederick Muller, London: 1949) p56

[19] Richard Findlater, *Lilian Baylis* (Allen Lane, London: 1975), p160

[20] TM

[21] TM

Ariel in the tree

[1] Nina Auerbach, *Ellen Terry: Player in Her Time* (J M Dent, London: 1987) p371

[2] ET/*Memoirs*, p302

[3] TM

[4] ETMM

[5] ET/*Memoirs*, p300

[6] *Letters of Graham Robertson*, ed Kerrison Preston (Hamish Hamilton, London: 1953) p198

[7] *Letters of Graham Robertson*, ed Kerrison Preston (Hamish Hamilton, London: 1963) p199

[8] ETMM

[9] ETMM

[10] TM

[11] ET/*Memoirs*, pp175-6

Bibliography

Mrs J. Comyns Carr, Eve Adam (ed), *Mrs J. Comyns Carr's Reminiscences* (Hutchinson, London: 1928)

Eleanor Adlard (ed) *Edy* (Muller, London: 1949)

Mrs Aria, *My Sentimental Self* (Chapman & Hall, London: 1922)

Lena Ashwell, *Myself a Player* (Michael Joseph, London: 1936)

Nina Auerbach, *Ellen Terry: Player in Her Time* (J.M. Dent, London: 1987)

The Bancrofts, *Recollections of 60 Years* (John Murray, London: 1909)

Sir Frank Benson, *My Memoirs* (Ernest Benn, London: 1930)

Wilfrid Blunt, *England's Michelangelo a biography of George Frederic Watts* (Hamish Hamilton, London: 1975)

Ronald Chapman, *The Laurel and the* Thorn: *A Study of G.F. Watts* (Faber & Faber, London: 1945)

Katharine Cockin, 'Ellen Terry: The Ghost-Writer and the Laughing Statue: The Victorian Actress, Letters and Life-Writing' in *Journal of European Studies,* 2002)

Katharine Cockin, 'Slinging the Ink About: Ellen Terry and Women's Suffrage Agitation' in *Gender and Politics in the Age of Letter-Writing* (Ashgate Publishing, Hampshire: 2004)

Edward Craig, *Gordon Craig: The Story of His Life* (Victor Gollancz, London: 1968)

Edward Gordon Craig, *Index to the Story of My Days* (Hulton Press, London: 1957)

Edward Gordon Craig, *Ellen Terry and Her Secret Self* (Sampson Low, Marston, London: 1931)

Lady Duff Gordon, *Discretions and Indiscretions* (Jarrolds, London: 1932)

Malcolm Elwin, *Charles Reade* (Jonathan Cape, London: 1931)

Richard Findlater, *Lilian Baylis* (Allen Lane, London: 1975)

Sir Johnston Forbes-Robertson, *A Player Under Three Reigns* (T.Fisher Unwin, London: 1925)

Kate Terry Gielgud, *An Autobiography* (Max Reinhardt, London: 1953)

Roger Lancelyn Green (ed), *The Diaries of Lewis Carroll* (Cassell, London: 1930)

Dudley Harbron, *The Conscious Stone* (Latimer House, London: 1949)

Charles Hiatt, *Ellen Terry* (George Bell, London: 1899)

Laurence Irving, *Henry Irving: The Actor and His World* (Columbus, London: 1989)

David Loshak, 'G.F. Watts and Ellen Terry' in *The Burlington Magazine* November 1963

Roger Manvell, *Ellen Terry* (William Heinemann, London: 1968)

Joy Melville, *Ellen and Edy* (Pandora Press, London: 1987)

Blanche Patch, *Thirty Years with GBS* (Victor Gollancz, London: 1951)
Tom Prideaux, *Love or Nothing: The Life and Times of Ellen Terry* (Millington Books, London: 1975)

T. Edgar Pemberton, *Ellen Terry and Her Sisters* (Arthur Pearson, London: 1902)

Margot Peters, *Bernard Shaw and the Actresses* (Doubleday, New York: 1980)

Kerrison Preston (ed), *Letters from Graham Robertson* (London: Hamish Hamilton, 1975)

Charles L. Reade and the Reverend Compton Reade, *Charles Reade* (Chapman & Hall, London: 1887)

Christopher St John, *Hungerheart: The Story of a Soul* (Methuen, London: 1915)

Mrs Clement Scott, *Old Days in Bohemian London* (Frederick A. Stokes, New York: 1919)

Henry Silver's Diary, mss *Punch Publications*

Marguerite Steen, *A Pride of Terrys* (Longmans, London: 1962)

A.M.W. Stirling, *Life's Little Day* (Butterworth, London: 1924)

Ellen Terry and Bernard Shaw: A Correspondence, ed Christopher St John (Constable, London: 1931)

Ellen Terry, *Ellen Terry's Memoirs* with preface, notes and additional biographical chapters by Edith Craig and Christopher St John (Victor Gollancz, London: 1933)

Ellen Terry, 'Stray Memories' in *The New Review*, Nos 23-25, 1891

Margaret Webster, *The Same Only Different* (Victor Gollancz, London: 1969)

Acknowledgements

The author and publisher wish to thank the National Trust and staff of Ellen Terry Museum, Smallhythe, Kent for the illustrations.

Index

A

Ailsa Craig, 107, 115
Aix-Les-Bains, 173
Alexandra, Queen, 187
Allingham, William, 232
Aria, Mrs, 163, 233
Arnold, Sir Edwin, 81
Arts Club, 72
Ashwell, Lena, 204
Atwood, Clare (Tony), 219, 230, 234
Auerbach, Nina, 224
Austin, Louis Frederick, 123, 127–8
Aynesworth, Alan, 105

B

Bach, J S, 55
Baltimore, 122
Bancroft, Mrs, 21–2, 72–4, 76–7, 81, 130
Bancroft, Sir Squire, 21–2, 72, 75–7, 81, 130, 224–6
Barney (Hilda Barnes), 223, 228–232
Barrie, J M, 175, 188, 212, 224-6
Bateman, Colonel, 90
Bateman, Mrs, 91
Bath, 9, 27, 189, 224–6
Bath Buns, 193
Baylis, Lilian, 217–19
Beethoven, Ludwig van, 44
Beggarstaff Brothers, 91
Behenna, Mary, 89
Behnes, William, 31
Belfast, 23
Benson, Frank, 96
Berlin, 135, 188

Bernhardt, Sarah, 45, 95, 97, 113, 214
Bertha (maid), 215
Birmingham, 98
Blake, William, 81
Blunt, Wilfrid, 37
Bo (Miss Bocking), 71, 80, 233
Boer War, 171
Booth, Edwin, 93, 110, 119
Boston, 122, 129, 134
Boucicault, Dion, 46, 90
Bournemouth, 164
Bramly, Bertha, 131
Brereton, Austin, 193
Bristol, 23–5, 27, 32, 52–4, 134
British Ideal Film company, 216
Brodribb, Samuel, 89
Brooks, Shirley, 36
Brough brothers, 24
Browning, Robert, 38
Burges, William, 56
burlesques, 21–2, 101
Burnett, Mrs Hodgson, 195
Byron, H J, 124

C

Caldecott, Randolph, 81
Calmour, Alfred, 134
Calvert, Charles, 77
Cameron, Julia Margaret, 30–1, 37–8, 40
Campbell, Lady Archibald, 131
Campbell, Mrs Patrick, 193
Cardiff Castle, 57
Carew, James, 8, 192–6, 198, 209, 215; separation from ET, 123, 228; and ET's last years, 223, 228; and ET's funeral, 233
Carroll, Lewis, 8, 19–20, 39, 45–6,

85, 106

Caruso, Enrico, 193

Charlie (dog), 129, 132

Charrington, Mr and Mrs, 160

Chase, Pauline, 189

Chesterton, G K, 42

Chicago, 41, 105, 122, 128, 134, 137, 150, 157, 192

Churchill, Lady Randolph, 169

Churchill, Winston, 192

Chute, James Henry, 23, 25, 27

Cincinnati, 122

Cockin, Katharine, 210

Coghlan, Charles, 76

Coleridge, Stephen, 128

Columbus, 122

Comédie Française, 97

Comyns Carr, Alice, 75, 126, 131–2, 141, 144

Comyns Carr, Joe, 126, 132, 141, 151

Cook, Dutton, 18, 22

Cooper, Frank, 158, 163

Cornwall, 89

Coventry, 15

Craig, Deirdre, 199

Craig, Edith (Edy), 102, 108, 154; birth and childhood, 58, 60–3, 65, 71, 74–5; and end of parents' relationship, 77–81, 131; and ET's marriage to Kelly, 83–4; stage debut, 85; on ET, 54, 97, 105; takes Craig name, 103, 107, 115; and Tennyson, 109; education and time in Germany, 115, 135, 141, 144–5, 147; receives advice on drawing, 128–9; and Godwin's death, 131; appears in *Faust*, 133;

christening, 134; stage career, 135, 148, 156–8, 160–1, 163, 176, 178, 187–8, 193–4, 203, 215, 216–17; American tour, 136–7; home life, 142; relations with ET, 157–8, 161, 163–4, 170, 172–3, 180–3, 197, 199; character, 158; relationship with Chris St John, 169–70, 172–3, 175, 219; relations with Ted, 180–2; relationship with Martin Shaw, 180–1, 183, 197; sexuality, 183; living at Smallhythe, 197, 219; and ET's third marriage, 194–5, 196; and women's movement, 203, 211–12; and ET's lectures, 206; and ET's last years, 209, 223–6, 227, 228–232; death, 232

Craig, Edward Gordon (Teddy), 64, 102, 131; birth and childhood, 60–3, 71, 74–5; and end of parents' relationship, 77–81, 114; and ET's marriage to Kelly, 84–5; stage debut, 85, 124; on ET, 93, 96–7, 105–6, 109, 141–2; takes Craig name, 103, 107, 115; education and time in Germany, 114–15, 129–30, 135–7, 141; visits New York, 128–9; and Godwin's death, 131; stage career, 146–7, 149, 171, 176–7, 178–9, 187–8; marriage and family, 149–51, 164, 180, 204; relations with ET, 172–3; relations with Edy, 180–2; reunited with ET, 209; mounts theatre arts and crafts exhibition, 221; and ET's last years, 209, 212, 228–230, 233

Craig, Edward, 78, 130, 204

249